Exploring the Yorkshire Dales

by Edward Gower

DALESMAN BOOKS
1980

THE DALESMAN PUBLISHING COMPANY LTD.
CLAPHAM (via Lancaster), NORTH YORKSHIRE

First published 1975
Second edition 1976
Third edition 1978
Fourth edition 1980

Front cover drawing of Kilnsey by Alec Wright

ISBN: 0 85206 603 1

Printed in Great Britain by
GEORGE TODD & SON
Marlborough Street, Whitehaven

Contents

Introduction

THERE are scores of dales within the traditional boundaries of Yorkshire, but to many people the 'Yorkshire Dales' means the vast area of open country which includes the 680 square miles of the Yorkshire Dales National Park. Practically all of this area is in the county of North Yorkshire, created in April 1974 and the largest county in England for acreage but with a population of only 645,000. In the Dales is some of the finest limestone terrain in Britain. There is a diversity of moors, mountains, rivers, lakes and attractive old villages. For the walker, climber, geologist, botanist, naturalist and historian, there is much of interest. For the tourist, there are many scenic routes and quiet roads, with hospitality offered in most of the villages.

There are five main dales — Swale, Wensley, Wharfe, Nidd and Ribble — as well as the Three Peaks district of north-west Craven, and the Aire valley in Craven based on Skipton. Nidderdale is not in the National Park, but is equally fine in scenery and probably the least visited. There is little industry in the Yorkshire Dales apart from farming and limestone extraction, which because of the increase in size during the last few years has caused controversy. However, the lime works are unlikely to spoil a visitor's pleasure, and may even pass unnoticed.

The Yorkshire Dales National Park

The National Park was established in 1954. Most of the land is privately owned, and visitors using footpaths and traversing open moorland should respect this fact and avoid damaging crops, walls and fences. Most farmers and land-owners welcome visitors so long as they remember much of the countryside provides someone's livelihood. Footpath information can be found on the map-boards displayed in many of the villages and tourist areas.

Weather information for the Three Peaks area is available at weekends from the **Penyghent Cafe** in Horton-in-Ribblesdale; Clapham Information Centre; and Ingleton Police Station.

Ordnance Survey 1:50,000 map Sheet 98, covers most of the area. Adjacent sheets are Nos. 91, 99, 103, 104. The 2½-inch to the mile maps can be obtained to cover the whole area. The Dalesman Yorkshire Dales Map (½-inch to the mile) is useful. Guide books to separate districts and dales, published by the Dalesman Publishing Company Ltd., Clapham, Lancaster, are on sale in many centres in the National Park.

National Park Centres are situated at Malham (tel. Airton 363); Clapham (tel. Clapham 419); Grassington (tel. 752748); Aysgarth Falls car park (tel. Aysgarth 424); Hawes (tel. Hawes 450); and Sedbergh (tel. Sedbergh 20125).

There are six full time National Park wardens, a number of part time assistants and about sixty volunteer wardens who are mainly active at weekends. The headquarters of the National Park Information Service is at 'Colvend,' Grassington, Skipton, North Yorkshire, and postal enquiries should be addressed there (tel. 752748).

Dales Rail, operated on the first weekend of each month from April to October, runs from Leeds to Carlisle, with small stations opened for walkers. Details from National Park Information Service, Colvend, Grassington, Skipton.

Warning: Although the mountains are not as high as those in the Lake District or Wales, they can be just as dangerous. Low cloud and mist can form with little warning, and bogs are common. Carry waterproofs, extra sweaters, and wear boots. Map and compass are essential, as is some emergency food. Make sure someone knows where you are going, and give some idea of your expected return time. In many parts of the upper dale, old mine shafts can be a hazard. The parts affected most are in Upper Wharfedale and Swaledale. Approach shafts with care, do not try to explore underground, and keep away from them in mist, snow or stormy weather.

The Pennine Way.   This 250 mile long-distance footpath passes through the Yorkshire Dales National Park. Full details are given in the Dalesman book *The Pennine Way* by Kenneth Oldham.

Caves and Potholes.   There are scores of these. They are dangerous and should not be entered unless taking part in an organised expedition with an established club. Show caves open to the public which do not require special clothing or equipment, are: Stump Cross Cavern, between Grassington and Pateley Bridge, at Greenhow — open daily. White Scar Cave, near Ingleton, on Hawes road — open daily. Ingleborough Cave, near Clapham (1 mile walk from village) — open daily in summer.

Angling. Many of the Dales rivers and streams have fish, but most of the water is in private hands or is controlled by clubs. Permission must be obtained from the holders of the fishing rights, some of whom issue day or weekly tickets. A rod licence is always required.

Caravans. Sites for tourist vans are listed in the text. T indicates Trailer. MC indicates Motor Caravan.

Further Information. Information, including details of accommodation, may be obtained from: The Yorkshire, Cleveland and Humberside Tourist Board, 312 Tadcaster Road, York YO2 2HF (20p).

The Yorkshire Dales Tourist Association, Burnsall, Skipton BD23 6BP (tel. Burnsall 668). Guide (£1) and postage.

Swaledale: Tourist Information Service, Richmond, North Yorkshire (15p).

The Public Relations Officer, North Yorkshire County Council, County Hall, Northallerton (35p).

Swaledale

THE most northerly of the main dales, Swaledale takes its name from the fast flowing river Swale. Richly wooded at the lower end, its upper reaches are wild and rugged, with great hills often called 'seats' (from the Norwegian 'saeters') and several spectacular waterfalls. For centuries, the dale was a lead-mining centre, but the ghostly ruins now absorbed in the landscape are all that remain. Wool was the foundation of the dale's prosperity, and large flocks of the Swaledale sheep are scattered on the high slopes at all times of the year. The solid stone outbarns linked by straggling stone walls catch the eye, and the old farmhouses, often in sheltered hollows, have a windbreak of trees.

RICHMOND

11m Leyburn, B6271, B6274, A6108. 3m A1 (Scotch Corner).

The only community of any size in the dale, Richmond is probably one of the most attractive small towns in northern England. Unlike other dales centres, it has many russet coloured pantiled roofs akin to the villages of the North York Moors. It is near the A1, at Scotch Corner, and the main railway is at Darlington 12 miles away. United buses serve Richmond, with limited services up the dale as far as Keld. The Pennine Way crosses Swaledale near Keld.

A cave below Richmond Castle is reputed to be the resting place of King Arthur and the Knights of the Round Table. The Castle (open daily), high on the river bank, was commenced by Alan Rufus, and the great keep, 100 feet high and built on top of the gatehouse, gives a fine viewpoint of the town and countryside. The cobbled market place has a tall cross erected in 1771, and on one side the ancient Holy Trinity church used to have shops incorporated. Now it

7

SWALEDALE and ARKENGARTHDALE

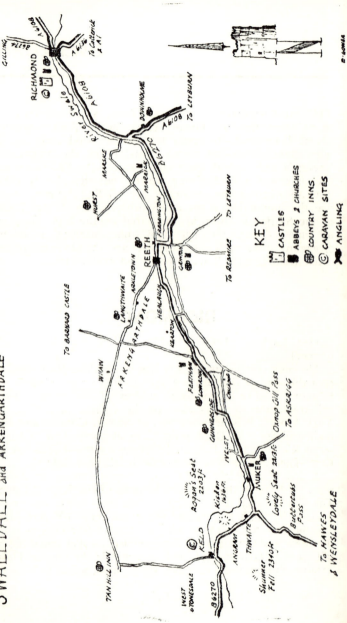

KEY

- 🏰 CASTLES
- ⛪ ABBEYS & CHURCHES
- Ⓘ COUNTRY INNS.
- Ⓒ CARAVAN SITES
- 🎣 ANGLING

houses the Regimental Museum of the Green Howards (open daily). On the south side is the Town Hall, dated 1756.

Castle Hill leads to the Bar, an arch in the town wall, and after passing Georgian houses the Green is reached and the river bridge. This fine structure was built in 1789 by John Carr. Finkle Street leads from the square to Newbiggin, a wide street with trees and fine houses, and to Temple Lodge, built in 1764. In the grounds is Culloden Tower, commemorating the Jacobite defeat. Friars Wynd, in the Market Place, gives access to the Theatre Royal, one of the oldest and best preserved Georgian theatres in England. This is open to visitors between May and September, daily. Frenchgate has some wealthy houses of the Georgian period, and in Pottergate is Hill House, the home of Francis I'anson, who is famous as the 'Sweet Lass of Richmond Hill.'

St. Mary's church has a tower built in 1400 but the main building was extensively restored in 1860. Greyfriars, in Queens Road, has a slender tower and Franciscan connections. J. M. W. Turner made several drawings of Richmond. The old railway station, built in 1848, has been converted into a garden centre and the engine shed into a public hall.

Shops: There are some good shops and several cafes, garages, banks, inns and hotels.

Market Day: Saturday.

Early Closing: Wednesday.

Caravan Sites: Swale View Caravan Park, Reeth Road, T, MC. Hargill House, Gilling West (3m B6274), T, MC. Round Howe (National Trust), picnic site and caravan site. King William IV, Barton.

Tourist Information Service, Friary Gardens, Queens Road. Tel. 0748 3525.

Swimming Baths (tel. 4581).

Buses: United, from Darlington, Leyburn, Hawes.

Angling: Day and weekly permits from Mr. W. Metcalfe, Market Place, Richmond.

Golf Club.

Easby Abbey. 1m east of Richmond. This picturesque ruin was founded by the Constable of Richmond Castle in 1155 for the Premonstratensian canons. There is a gatehouse, and a parish church in the precincts. A pleasant riverside walk leads from Richmond to the abbey.

Marske. 5m Richmond, off the B6270. A small village set in trees above the river, it has the church of St. Edmund with an ancient double bellcote and Norman doorways. A footpath from Richmond passes through a ravine and under Whitcliffe Scar. At Willances Leap, memorial stones commemorate the escape of Robert Willance when his horse leapt down the slope. Marske Hall, once the seat of the Hutton family, has some fine landscaped gardens. West of the village is an obelisk to a member of the family.

Post Office.

Downholme. On the A6108 Leyburn road, this village has a Norman church and a fine bridge over the Swale, built by Carr. 1½m to the SE is Walburn Hall, a fortified Elizabethan house.

Inn: Bolton Arms.
Post Office.

Marrick Priory. Off the Marske to Reeth road. The Benedictine priory has a spectacular and rather difficult approach by way of 365 steps. The ruins now incorporate a hostel for youth organisations. The church of St. Andrew was probably built from priory materials. There is also a footpath from the road near Fremington, further up the river. Riverside car park, from Fremington.

Ellerton Abbey. The ruins of a Cistercian nunnery are across the river from Marrick, once reached by stepping stones. They can be seen from the Richmond to Grinton road.

Hurst. 2½m north from the Marske-Reeth road, opposite road to Marrick. Around the hamlet are lead-mining hillocks, reminders of an industry that occupied the local population for 18 centuries, and closed down around 1890. A pig of smelted lead found here bore the inscription of the Roman Emperor Hadrian (117-138 A.D.).

Inn: The Green Dragon.

Fremington. B6270, 10m from Richmond. High and Low Fremington lie under a great 'Edge' or scar, from which chert was once quarried for the Potteries. The valley, wide and flat bottomed here, is crossed by the bridge to Grinton.

Grinton. B6270. The parish covers 49,000 acres, of which 30,000 are moorland. It has a church which is now too big for the population of 100 or so. In the 19th century there were 700 inhabitants. The church, of Norman origin, was part of the manor, which, until the Dissolution in 1538 belonged to Bridlington Priory. To its graveyard the dead of the dale were for many centuries carried by the Corpse Way. This trod, used by prehistoric man, runs from Keld and Muker on the north slope of the dale. The bodies were carried in wicker baskets. After the new chapel at Muker was consecrated in 1580, corpses from above Gunnerside were taken there. In 1716 the curate at Muker refused to bury corpses without coffins. Above Grinton, on the road to Wensleydale, is Grinton Lodge, once a shooting lodge and now a youth hostel. There are more lead-mining relics on Grinton Moor.

Inn: Bridge Inn.
Post Office.

Reeth. B6270, 11m from Richmond. Standing at the junction with Arkengarthdale, Reeth is the centre for mid-Swaledale. Its bridge spans Arkle Beck, which joins the Swale in rich flat grassland. Fine old stone houses are grouped round a wide green. The village was once an important market town and lead-mining centre, and there are several old inns. Pleasant walks are in abundance. Maiden Castle, an ancient earthwork, lies across the valley on Harkerside. Trees in the area include yew and juniper.

Inns: King's Arms. Black Bull. Buck. Burgoyne Hotel.
Garages: Two.
Several shops, cafes and banks.
Early closing day: Thursday. Agricultural show in September.
Buses: United buses from Richmond.

Healaugh. This cluster of well-kept cottages a mile or so above Reeth has no inn or shop, but does have a chapel. Half of the manor was bought from the crown in 1556 by Lord Wharton, the owner of the manor of Muker. The Whartons built Park Hall, near the village, on the lane to Kearton. Wild deer once roamed the district.

Post Office.

Feetham. B6270. This village links with long straggling Low Row and a road joins it with Arkengarthdale. Behind it rear two great fells, Rogans Seat and Great Pinseat. The parish church, Holy Trinity, was built in 1810, and the Congregational chapel the year before.

Inn: The Punchbowl.

Low Row. Non-conformity started in the upper dale at nearby Blades. William Spensley made a cottage into a chapel and John Wesley visited it. The Quakers had a meeting house A short distance up the dale from Low Row, a bridge spanning the Swale carries a road leading to the hamlet of Crackpot. This is a Norse name for a deep hole frequented by carrion crows.

Inn: King's Head.
Bank. Post Office.
Fishing: Day permits from M. Stockwell, 93 George Street, Thornaby.

Gunnerside. B6270, 17m from Richmond. The beck in the village runs off Rogans Seat and into the Swale, which has a wide floor here. This is a large village, developed during lead-mining days. The name comes from a Norseman called Gunner. The stone houses cluster under the fellside, and the quiet street must have been a bustling scene in the 18th century, with miners, blacksmiths, wagon-drivers and the farmers congregating. The decline of lead-mining caused many people to leave the dale and seek work in the industrial towns of Lancashire. Their kinsfolk still return to the village, to fill the large chapel at the Mid-summer Festival. The riverside between Gunnerside and Low Row has several popular picnic spots, such as Rowleth Woods.

Shops: Post Office. Stores.
Inn: King's Head.

Muker. B6270, 20m from Richmond. Also approached by minor road from Askrigg in Wensleydale (steep climb). A cluster of stone and slate, the village stands on its beck, which joins the Swale a short distance down the dale. On the hillside is the church of St. Mary, built in 1580 to serve a huge area with a small population. There is a tiny green and steep alleys and steps. There used to be three inns, which were filled with merry dalesfolk when the four day festival called 'T'aud Roy' was held around Christmas. There was a market on the green. The Literary Institute was built about 1868 and its prominent gable is attractive. Richard and Cherry Kearton, pioneers of wild life photography, attended the school, as the tablets next to the door commemorate. Muker Show is held in September.

Inn: Farmer's Arms.
Village Stores. Post 'Office. Bank.
Petrol.

Between Muker and the next village, Thwaite, is the road to the left climbing to the Buttertubs Pass, between Shunner Fell (2,340 feet) and Lovely Seat (2,213 feet). At the roadside are 58 deep shafts in the limestone, made by acidified water enlarging the clints. The spectacular road leads to Hawes in Wensleydale.

Thwaite. B6270. This old village has a bridge over the same beck as Muker, but here called Thwaite Beck. The Kearton brothers were born here, sons of a shepherd.

Pennine Way: No. 11 on map.
Kearton Guest House and Shop.

Passing through the highest village in the dale, Angram (1,185 feet), the road approaches:

Keld. Lying just off the dale road to the right, this cluster of old stone houses around a tiny square is near the main river, which skirts the great hill called Kisdon. The approach road is narrow, and car parking is limited. The name Keld comes from a Norse word for water spring. This is fine walking country — the Pennine Way passes close by — and there is a youth hostel just above the village on the B6270. A footpath leads from the Square into a gorge, with Cat-rake Foss and Kisdon Foss not far down. Foss, or Force, means waterfall.

Shop and Post Office.
Hope House Filling Station and Camping Site.
United buses from Richmond.

A short distance upstream is another waterfall, Wainwath Foss, but before this, at Park Bridge, a steep narrow road leads off to the right to West Stonesdale and England's highest inn.

Tan Hill. At 1,732 feet, this lonely house looks over miles of wild moorland. Coal was once mined here, and used in the Swaledale lead-mines. In the 18th century boxing contests drew crowds, but today's attraction, at the end of May, is the annual sheep fair. The Swaledale breed of sheep was started in this area. The road from the inn eastwards runs into Arkengarthdale and Reeth.

The B6270 from Keld leads to Birkdale and Kirkby Stephen, which until April 1974 was in Westmorland but is now in the new county of Cumbria.

Arkengarthdale. From Reeth, to the north-west, is wide, grassy and lonely Arkengarthdale, with Arkle Beck flowing through it to the Swale. Lead-mining has left its scars, and trees are scarcer now than in the old days when wolves and boars hunted in the forest. The names of the hamlets are intriguing — Booze, Arkle Town and Whaw. The church is at Langthwaite, but has no long history. Charles Bathurst, lord of the manor in the 18th century, developed the lead-mining industry and the name of the hotel at Langthwaite, 'CB,' refers to him. The old Powder House is an interesting relic.

Inns: 'CB' and Red Lion.
Shop and Post Office.
Limited bus service from Reeth on weekdays.

South of Arkle is Calver Hill (pronounced 'cawver') from which chert was quarried. The road over the moor, a mile or so beyond Langthwaite, is the old route to Barnard Castle (14½m) which was used by 'jagger' ponies loaded with lead. Cheeses made in the upper dale were also taken to Barnard Castle market.

BOOKS

Mines and Miners of Swaledale, Arthur Raistrick (Dalesman).

Adam Brunskill, Thomas Armstrong.

Swaledale (Dalesman).

Yorkshire: North Riding, Oswald Harland (Hale).

Yorkshire: The North Riding, Malcolm Barker (Batsford).

Lead Mining in the Yorkshire Dales, Arthur Raistrick (Dalesman).

The Lead Mines of Wensleydale and Swaledale, Arthur Raistrick, 2 vols. (Moorland Publishing Co.).

Life and Tradition in the Yorkshire Dales, Hartley and Ingilby (Dent).

James Herriot's Yorkshire (Michael Joseph).

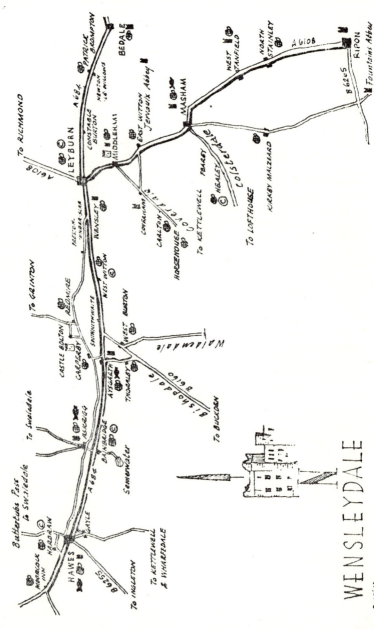

WENSLEYDALE

Wensleydale

Including Bishopdale, Waldendale, Coverdale and Colsterdale

THE largest of the dales, Wensleydale is wide and fertile in its lower regions and wild and spectacular at its head. Taking its name from the village of Wensley, the dale has the river Ure (originally Yore) flowing through it from Abbotside near the border with Cumbria. Several small dales branch from the valley, which has splendid castles, a ruined abbey, waterfalls, a lake and many attractive villages. The two main towns, Hawes in the upper dale and Leyburn in the middle, are good centres. Masham is the centre of the lower dale and the ancient cathedral city of Ripon marks the start of the dale country. Fountains Abbey is near Ripon. Wensleydale cheese is known all over the north. Racehorses are bred in Middleham, where a king once lived, and at Castle Bolton a famous queen was imprisoned. The Wensleydale longwool sheep is widespread in the north.

HAWES

A684 from Leyburn (east) or Sedbergh (west); B6255 from Ingleton. Minor roads from Kettlewell (1,934 feet, highest road in Yorkshire) and from Swaledale (Buttertubs Pass).

The capital of the upper dale, Hawes has a market on Tuesdays. It was once served by rail from Northallerton, but the line was closed in 1959. United buses link with Leyburn, Darlington, Ripon and Richmond, and Ribble buses run to Sedbergh and Kendal. There are West Yorkshire buses from Bradford at summer weekends.

The name comes from the Anglo-Saxon 'haus' meaning a mountain pass. Although the area was first populated in

17

the 13th century, the town has few obvious antiquities. The auction mart is important, and at the lamb sales thousands of dales-born animals fill the street with their bleating. The market charter was granted in 1699, with the right to hold a fair in April and September. Previous to this Askrigg was the market centre but declined with the growth of Hawes as textile manufacture and quarrying were developed.

A fine centre for walking, Hawes is on the Pennine Way (No. 10 on Pennine Way Map). The road into Wharfedale climbs nearly 2,000 feet to Fleet Moss, with panoramic views of the dales, and is crossed by a Roman road from Bainbridge to Ribblehead. Great hills encircle the town—Dodd Fell, Widdale Fell and Brough Fell, all over 2,000 feet.

The church of St. Margaret, perched above the town, was built in 1851 and has an interesting black marble font. The Market Hall is dated 1902. Seventeenth century houses, with dated doorheads, can be seen in the intricate streets.

There are several inns, shops, banks, places of worship, garages and cafes. There is a museum in the Station Yard.

Youth Hostel.

National Park Information Centre and car park: Station Yard.

Population: Around 800.

Early Closing Day: Wednesday. Market Day: Tuesday.

Sports and Gala in June.

Caravan Sites: Bainbridge Ings Caravan Site (off A684), T, MC. Brown Moor, T, MC. The Greens Caravan Site, T, MC. (A684). Honeycott Caravan Site, T, MC (B6265).

Angling: Tickets from Miss M. Thwaite, Mount View, Hawes.

Pony Trekking: Sedbusk (1½m).

Gayle. Linked with Hawes, Gayle is an intricate jumble of old stone buildings, divided by Duerly Beck which is often noisy with ducks and geese. Two waterfalls, Gayle Force and Aisgill, are in the village. One house has a decorated door lintel dated 1695, and the old cotton mill, with three storeys, was built in 1784. The road up the hill from the beck, crossed by both bridge and ford, is the Fleet Moss climb to Wharfedale. Wensleydale cheese is made at the factory on the outskirts. Until the 1930s this was a farmhouse industry, the cheese originally being produced from ewes' milk by the monks of Jervaulx Abbey, lower down the dale. There is a bus service to Ripon.

Cotterdale. A tiny community with a small barn-like chapel, Cotterdale is approached by turning right off the A684 between Hawes and Garsdale Head.

Appersett. A hamlet standing at the junction of the Ure and Widdale Beck. It takes its name, together with nearby Burtersett and Countersett, from the Norse word 'saeter,' a mountain pasture.

Burtersett. Lies off the main dale road a mile or so below Hawes. The road from it twists and climbs, crossing the Roman road and dropping into:

Countersett. Overlooks the large expanse of Semerwater. From there the road leads to Stalling Busk, with its tiny church.

Semerwater. Drained by England's shortest river, the Bain (2 miles long), Semerwater is a popular place for sailing and water ski-ing. On its shores are huge boulders of Shap granite left by glaciers.
A legend tells of a city under the water — drowned because its inhabitants refused hospitality to a beggar. There were lake dwellings here in 1000 B.C. Semerwater is also reached by a road from Bainbridge (2½m).

Angling: Day tickets from Low Blean Farm (300 yards past lake).

Bainbridge. A684, 4m from Hawes. On the hill overlooking the village are the remains of a Roman fort, Virosidium. The road from Bainbridge to Stalling Busk eventually climbs to the Stake Pass, over which the Roman soldiers tramped on their way to Ilkley (pedestrians only beyond Stalling Busk). The houses at Bainbridge are grouped round a large green and two 18th century river bridges. The old stocks are on the green, and a 'forest horn' blown three times each evening from September 28 to Shrovetide is kept at the Rose and Crown Inn, which dates from 1445. There is no church, but a chapel built in 1864 is close to the green, as is the village school. Less than a mile away, across the Ure (Yore Bridge) is Coleby Hall, dated 1633, a fine three-gabled manor house.

Petrol Station: Woodhall, 2m on Askrigg road.
Inn: Rose and Crown.
Shop and Post Office. Garage.
Caravans: Bainbridge Ings Caravan Site, T, MC (off A684).
Angling: Tickets from The Rose and Crown Inn.
Buses from Hawes and Leyburn.

Worton. Has a 17th century Hall.

Inn: Victoria Arms.

Hardraw. 1¼m from Hawes. On north side of river Ure — turn left at T-junction after crossing river from Hawes. The Green Dragon Inn gives access to **Hardraw Force, a** waterfall **98** feet high and reputed to be the deepest unbroken fall in England. The footpath from the inn follows a little valley which used to be the scene of brass band concerts — these have recently been revived. The road near Hardraw ascends the Buttertubs Pass into Swaledale.

Inn: Green Dragon. Caravan Site.

Askrigg. A large village, Askrigg was once an important market centre with annual fairs and was famed for its clockmakers. It had a textile industry and in the 17th century a lot of hand-knitters. Near the church is part of a cross, and a cylindrical stone pump. There are several houses with decorated and dated lintels of the 17th and 18th centuries. One of the finest in North Yorkshire the church of St. Oswald is Late Perpendicular. It has a chantry founded by James Metcalfe of Nappa Hall in 1467, and a nave ceiling with massive moulded beams.

Inns: Crown. King's Arms.
Shop. Garage at Woodhall (2m).
Youth Centre: Low Mill.
Angling: Tickets from the King's Arms Hotel.
Caravan Site: Carr End (night halt).
Buses from Hawes and Leyburn.

Nappa Hall, 1½m east of Askrigg, is a fortified manor house built by Thomas Metcalfe around 1460. It is a fine building screened by a monkey puzzle tree, but little of the original interior remains. The Metcalfes were an important family in Wensleydale for centuries. Thomas led the Wensleydale Archers to Agincourt.

Aysgarth. A684, 9½m from Hawes, 7½m from Leyburn. Famed for its waterfalls, Aysgarth has a church with the largest graveyard in the dales. The village stands well above the river, but a road leads down to the 16th century bridge giving a view of the High Force. Lower down are two more spectacular falls reached by footpaths. There is a car park north of the river near the old railway station, and another on the south side. Yore Mill, near the bridge, is now a museum for old carriages, etc. (open daily 10-00 to 6-00). The church of St. Andrew, near the river, is a large one but only the tower is old. There are two interesting screens.

Inns: George and Dragon. Palmer Flatt. Falls Motel.
Garage, Shop and Post Office. Youth Hostel.
National Park Information Centre: Falls Car Park.
Aysgarth Falls Nature Trail.
Buses from Hawes, Leyburn and Darlington.

Carperby. Across the river from Aysgarth. Old cottages and farms line the road, and there is a small green. The village cross has seven steps and dates from 1674. There is a Friends Meeting House and a Methodist chapel. The village has a reputation for tidiness.

Inn: Wheatsheaf.
Post Office and Stores.
Petrol: Woodhall (2m on Askrigg road).
Buses from Hawes and Leyburn.

Castle Bolton. 2m Carperby, 5m Leyburn. Although ruinous inside, this massive castle retains its exterior fairly complete. There are four mighty towers, of four storeys, with three-storey living quarters round an enclosed court-yard. Built in 1379 by Richard Scrope, the castle combined defence with domestic comfort, and was besieged by Par-liamentary forces in 1645. Mary, Queen of Scots, was imprisoned in it for a time, and there are rooms which she is said to have used open to the public. There is a small museum, and a restaurant inside the buildings.
The village, a straggle of old cottages flanking an area of grass, was for many years the home of the Dales artist,

Fred Lawson. The church of St. Oswald, in the shadow of the castle, is late 14th century. There is a car park with toilets adjacent to the castle.

Castle Opening Hours: Daily 10-00 to 6-30. Closed Mondays.
Post Office.
Buses from Hawes and Leyburn.

Redmire. 1m Castle Bolton. Standing well back from the river, Redmire was once busy with lead-miners. There is a ford across the Ure, and a waterfall near where the beck from Apedale, high on the moor, runs into the river. Half a mile south of the village is the small Norman church of St. Mary.

Inns: Bolton Arms. King's Arms.
Post Office and Store.
Caravan Site: Elm House (off A684), T.
Buses from Hawes and Leyburn.

Preston under Scar. The village, on the road to Leyburn from Redmire, has a medieval manor house.

Buses from Hawes and Leyburn pass the lane end.

Swinithwaite. A864. Its name means a clearing used for feeding pigs. Temple Farm, on the roadside, has a carved doorhead dated 1608. The dale, broad and fertile here, is colourful in autumn. The hall was built in 1767, and in the grounds is a temple dated 1792. On the other side of the Aysgarth road, a signpost leads to the Templar's Chapel, but only a few courses of masonry are to be seen. The Knights Templar are supposed to have had an establishment in the area.

West Witton. A684. A long village on the dale road, West Witton was once thronged with lead-miners but is now busy with tourists. Pen Hill (1,792 feet) lies to the south of the village, from which a footpath leads to the summit. This was a beacon in Napoleonic days. The ancient ceremony of 'Burning old Bartle' is carried out on the first Saturday after St. Bartholomew's Day in late August. The small church of St. Bartholomew has Norman origins, but was largely rebuilt in 1876. Opposite the church is an old house with two oval windows.

Inns: Wensleydale Heifer. Fox and Hounds. Star Hotel.
Shops and Post Office.
Caravan Site: Chantry Caravan Site (off A684), T, MC.
Buses from Hawes and Leyburn.

Wensley. A684. The village from which the dale takes its name lies at the junction of the two dale roads and is the residence of the lord of the manor. The entrance gates to Bolton Hall (not open to the public) are opposite the inn. Lord Bolton is a descendant of the Scrope family who built Bolton Castle. The church of Holy Trinity is important; it was built in various stages from Norman times and the west tower was rebuilt in 1719. It is rich in furnishings, and has a carved screen from Easby Abbey behind an elaborate 17th century Scrope family pew. A road just across the river leads to Carlton in Coverdale.

Inn: Three Horse Shoes.
Post Office. Garages.
Buses from Hawes and Leyburn.

LEYBURN

A6108, A684, Hawes 17m, Richmond 11½m. Leyburn, the centre of the middle dale, is at the junction of five roads. It has a market charter since 1686 and the large market place is busy on Fridays. It also has a thriving auction mart for sheep and cattle. Little evidence of its ancient history is visible, the town hall in the market place being built in 1856. The church dates only from 1868, but Thornborough Hall — the old council offices — is Georgian, although altered in Victorian times. Leyburn Hall, just off the market place, is 18th century. The town is a good centre, with cafes and shops. Leyburn Shawl, between the town and Wensley, has seats and footpaths giving wide views of the countryside. Annual events include the Wensleydale Agricultural Show in September and the Wensleydale Tournament of Song.

Inns: King's Head. Bolton Arms. Black Swan. Golden Lion. Pheasant
Inn (Harmby 1m).

Garages.

Market Day: Friday. Early Closing: Wednesday.

Buses: United buses connect Leyburn with Hawes, Richmond, Ripon
and Darlington. West Yorkshire buses run from Bradford at
weekends in summer.

Population: 6,250.

Caravan Sites: Yorkshire Dales Caravan Park, Harmby, T. Akebar
Park (5m, A684), T, MC. Rosebar Caravan Site, T, MC.

Bellerby. A6108. There is an army camp near here and
firing ranges. The old hall is interesting.

Inn: Cross Keys.

Post Office and Shops.

Spennithorne. Near Leyburn, just off the A684 to Bedale,
this village has an interesting church with a 17th century
wall painting. There are monuments to the locally important
family of Van Straubenezee.

Middleham. A6108. An important 'town' rather than a
village, Middleham has a massive castle in which lived King
Richard III. After his death at Bosworth Field, the building
was robbed of its stones by local people and slighted by
Parliamentary order during the civil war. The keep, one of
the largest in England, still stands to its full height. Cared
for by the Department of the Environment, it is open daily.
There are two market crosses, one of them in the Swine
Market and several Georgian houses, including the Rectory.
The church, with the unusual dedication to St. Alkelda, dates
from the 14th century. The bridge over the river, originally
of suspension construction, is castellated and was built in
1829. Racehorses are bred in the town, a tradition going
back to the monks of Jervaulx Abbey. There is a footpath
on the riverside to Bishopdale Beck, below Aysgarth.

Population: Around 600.

Early Closing Day: Wednesday.

Inns: Commercial Hotel. Black Bull. White Swan. Black Swan.

Several shops. Cafe. Garage.

Road leads to Coverdale.

Buses from Hawes, Leyburn and Ripon.

East Witton. A6108, 2m Middleham. An attractive village, with its houses strung alongside a green. It once had an important market, until a plague in 1563 caused it to be moved. The church of St. John the Evangelist was built by the Earl of Ailesbury in 1809, together with the vicarage and some of the cottages. Ulshaw Bridge, between the village and Middleham, is a massive structure of 1674. Near to it is the church of St. Simon and St. Jude (1868) which lies behind a Georgian house. Slobbering Sal is a local name for a grotto on East Witton Fell. Braithwaite Hall, two miles on the Coverham road, is a fine old house of the mid-17th century. Near this is a rampart and ditch, the remains of a pre-Roman fort.

Inn: Coverbridge Inn.
Post Office and Shop.
Buses from Hawes, Leyburn and Ripon.

Jervaulx Abbey. Off A6108, 2m East Witton. Car park. Open daily dawn to dusk. Destroyed by Henry VIII and further damaged by local builders, the abbey ruins are still attractive. The Cistercian monks made the first Wensleydale cheese here from ewes' milk. The cloister is now a walled garden.

Buses from Hawes, Leyburn and Ripon.

Ellingstring. 2½m East Witton. Youth hostel.

Masham. A6108 from Ripon; also road to Kirkby Malzeard. The large market place has a cross in the middle, and a church with a tall spire at its edge. Still an important market town with busy sheep and cattle auctions, Masham gives its name to a well-known sheep crossbreed Swaledale X Wensleydale. Large fairs used to bring huge crowds of folk and animals. The main road skirts the market place, which allows plenty of parking space. St. Mary's church has a 15th century spire on top of a Norman tower. Masham is famous for its independent local brewery, which was started in 1827. Wensleydale cheese is also manufactured here. The grouse moors near the town are popular with sportsmen. A road leads from Masham over the moortops into Lofthouse in Nidderdale.

Inns: King's Head. Bay Horse. Bruce Arms. White Bear.
Cafes. Garages. Several shops.
Early Closing Day: Thursday.
There is a nine hole golf course. Tennis. Bowls.
Agricultural Show in September.
Traction Engine Rally in July.
United buses from Ripon, Leyburn, Hawes.

Druids Temple. A mock ruin built in 1820 to give work to local unemployed, it is a miniature Stonehenge. Reached by minor road to Swinton and Ilton (about 3m Masham).

Constable Burton. 3m Leyburn. Has a fine Georgian Hall built in 1762.

Bedale. 1½m A1 at Leeming; A684 from Leyburn. A pleasant market town with a wide cobbled main street, having a market cross. The church of St. Gregory, at the top of the street, has a 13th century nave and many interesting features including a wall painting and Dutch panelling. Bedale Hall is a fine Georgian building. There are several old three-storeyed houses and inns.

Market Day: Tuesday. Early Closing Day: Thursday.
Inns: Green Dragon. Waggon and Horses. King's Head. White
    Bear. Oddfellows' Arms.
Several shops, cafes, garages.
Buses from Darlington and Leyburn.

COLSTERDALE. A small quiet dale, drained by several becks and the river Burn, which runs into the Ure below Masham. The road from Masham leads to the villages of Fearby and Healey, then passes Leighton reservoirs and climbs to 1,400 feet before dropping into Nidderdale at Lofthouse. There are iron mine relics. Swinton Park is the seat of the Earl and Countess Swinton.

Inns: King's Head, Fearby. Black Swan, Healey.
Caravan Site: Fearby Caravan Site, T, MC.

COVERDALE. The river Cover drains this offshoot of Wensleydale and joins the Ure below Middleham. The road through the dale leads to Kettlewell, in Wharfedale, giving panoramic views and climbing to over 1,600 feet. It has a good surface but is steep and twisty in places. Access to the valley is from East Witton, Middleham and West Witton. There are several small villages — East Scrafton, West Scrafton, Melmerby, Carlton, Gammersgill and Horsehouse. **Coverham Abbey,** founded in the 13th century by the Premonstratensian order, is a small ruin in private grounds. Permission to view should be sought from the owners. Coverham church (Holy Trinity) is early 14th century but was restored in 1854. A well-known native of the dale was Miles Coverdale, the translator of the Scriptures and the 'Great Bible.' Carlton is a long roadside village, having several old houses with mullioned windows.

Inns: Forester's Arms, Carlton. Thwaite Arms, Horsehouse.
Garages: Carlton.

BISHOPDALE. B6160. Running south-west from Aysgarth, this dale links with Wharfedale via Kidstones Pass. Roads lead to it from below Aysgarth and from near Swinithwaite. The villages are at the lower end.

Thoralby. 1m Aysgarth, is a small village with several 17th century houses having mullioned windows. There is a shop and an inn, The George.

Newbiggin is a hamlet of old houses and farms, and lies off the main dale road on the hillside. At the road junction is the Street Head Inn, where there is a caravan site (T, MC).

WALDENDALE. A small quiet dale on the other side of Naughtberry Fell from Bishopdale, it has no through road for motors but is excellent walking country.

West Burton is at the foot of the dale. A charming village of old stone houses grouped round a green, it is across Bishopdale Beck from Thoralby. There is a waterfall behind the old mill at the bottom of the green. Above West Burton the road ceases after 3 miles.

Inn: Fox and Hounds.
Buses: From Richmond, Darlington, Leyburn and Hawes.

BOOKS

Bolton Castle (Dalesman). *Wensleydale* (Dalesman).

Dentdale, Sedbergh and Garsdale

DENTDALE is small and beautiful, an area of green meadows rising to high fells, with whitewashed farms dotted near the river Dee. It has only one village of importance, Dent, which is usually called a town. To the north is Rise Hill, and southwards is the great hump of Whernside, the highest of Yorkshire's Three Peaks. The Settle to Carlisle railway, one of Britain's most spectacular lines, runs at the eastern end of the valley. The now closed Dent station, reached by a steep road, stands wind-battered at more than 1,100 feet above sea level. The dale is connected with Sedbergh (A684 from Hawes) and by a road linking with the B6255 (Ingleton to Hawes road) at Newby Head.

From the B6255, the approach into Dentdale is under Dent Head viaduct, 100 feet high and 600 feet long. The railway has just emerged from Blea Moor tunnel. The road drops steeply to Lea Yeat, where the junction for Dent station turns to the right. The railway is perched up on the hillside, with Arten Gill viaduct preceding the station. In this section of the dale there is a youth hostel and the Sportsman's Inn. Near Arten Gill viaduct, the ruins of Stone House Marble Mill recall the industry which flourished in the dale in the 19th century. The marble was used for fireplace surrounds and monuments. The mill has a waterwheel 60 feet in diameter.

Cowgill. The Institute was originally a Quaker Meeting House. The church was built in 1837.

There is a narrow bridge over the river giving access to the road on the south side of the dale. The Dee, flowing over the smooth slabs of rock, submerges for a while, and appears at Hell Cauldron in a gorge. The dale below has an appearance more akin to Cumbria than Yorkshire. Some of the farmhouses, lying a field's length from the road, have

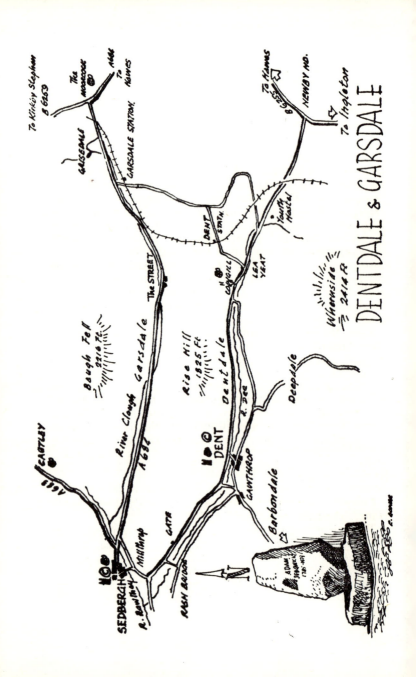

DENTDALE & GARSDALE

jutting chimney stacks, circular at the top. Gibbs Hall, now in ruins, was the home of William and Mary Howitt, Quaker authors. Deepdale Beck comes down from Whernside to join the Dee, and the road up this dale climbs to 1,500 feet to descend through Kingsdale into Ingleton. The dale roads converge on Dent.

Dent. Old houses line a cobbled street which twists and turns. The houses once had projecting galleries, under which clothes were dried. Water pours from under a huge granite slab, a memorial to Adam Sedgwick, who was born in Dent, a parson's son, in 1785. He became Canon of Norwich and a famous geologist, being made Woodwardian Professor of Geology. In the 17th and 18th centuries the town was a busy centre for knitwear. Huge quantities of stockings were supplied to the British army. All the members of the family knitted—even the shepherds as they walked their flocks to new pasture! Jerseys and coats were also knitted, and taken by cart to Kendal. St. Andrew's church has an old grammar school in its yard, the charter for which was granted by James I in 1603. The church was started in the early 13th century, but has been extensively restored, the tower being rebuilt about 1785.

Whernside Manor Cave and Fell Centre (National Park).

Inns: George and Dragon. Sun.

Shops: Garages, shops, cafe, post office.

Caravan and Camping Sites: High Laning Farm. Harborgill (Cowgill), tents.

Buses: To Sedbergh and Kendal (limited service).

Gawthrop. The village lies at the foot of the road over to Barbondale, about a mile below Dent. It is a tiny settlement with a green which was formerly a dam. The road on the south side of the river from Gawthrop is very narrow. Dentdale narrows below Dent and the main road down the valley crosses the river Rawthey into Sedbergh.

Sedbergh. A684, A683, 5m from Dent. An attractive market town with narrow streets frowned on by the Howgill Fells. Sedbergh was also busy once with knitters. The Quaker woollen mill at Hebblethwaite Hall is now a ruin. The railway, which brought some prosperity after 1861, is closed.

Sedbergh School is well known — from an original chantry school in 1525 it became a grammar school in 1716. The church of St. Andrew, of Norman origin, was restored in 1886. There are several Georgian houses.

There is an earth mound north-east of the town, Castlehaw Tower, which is thought to be of Roman origin. Behind the town is Winder (1,551 feet), from which there is a fine walk to the north to a hill called the Calf (2,220 feet), a fine view point. From there, eastwards is **Cautley Spout,** an impressive waterfall. This is more easily reached from the Sedbergh-Kirkby Stephen road (A683) at a point near the Cross Keys Temperance Hotel (4½m Sedbergh — garage and cafe near).

Market Day: Wednesday. Early Closing Day: Thursday.

Two car parks. Several shops and cafes. Cinema. Garages.

Inns: Bull. Red Lion. Golden Lion.

National Park Information Centre: 72 Main Street (tel. 20125).

Caravan Sites: Pinfold Caravan Site. Ingmire North Caravan Site, T. Cross Hall Farm, T, MC (2½m on Kirkby Stephen road, A683). Lincoln's Inn Caravan Site, Firbank, T, MC.

Angling: Tickets from E. Lowis, Main Street.

Buses to Kendal and Kirkby Lonsdale.

'Dales Rail' bus link with Hawes and Garsdale.

GARSDALE

A deep valley, on the north side of Rise Hill from Dentdale, it has the river Clough flowing through to join the Rawthey near Sedbergh. The road to it is from the Moorcock, on the A684 from Hawes. The now closed station on the Settle-Carlisle line, at the north side of Rise Hill tunnel from Dent, was originally the junction for the line down Wensleydale. There are no large centres. Garsdale Head has some railway buildings, and there is a hamlet called The Street, which has a church and two chapels.

Youth Hostel: Garsdale Head (Lunds).

Shop and Post Office.

Petrol. Also at Swarthgill.

Angling: Tickets from E. Lowis, Main Street, Sedbergh.

Ribblesdale and the Three Peaks

Including Settle, Ingleton and North Craven

THE river Ribble, although rising on the high fells near the source of the Wharfe, flows westwards, and in its lower parts is in Lancashire. The upper dale is splendid limestone country, with a great appeal to walkers and potholers. There are good centres, Settle and Ingleton, both on the A65. There is a National Park Information Centre at Clapham. South-west from Settle is the beautiful area known as the Forest of Bowland, with scenic drives and unspoilt villages.

Ribblehead. At the junction of the roads from Ingleton and Settle, Ribblehead is not a village. There is a lonely inn, a quarry and a massive railway viaduct, surrounded by mountains and wide moorland. The road continues to Hawes in Wensleydale. The viaduct has 24 arches and is 1,328 feet long. In the centre the height from foundation to rail is 105 feet. Winds have been known to stop trains. The now closed station was formerly a weather recording point for the Air Ministry. Church services used to be held in the tiny waiting room.

Inn: The Station.

On the west side of the railway is **Whernside** (2,414 feet), the highest of Yorkshire's Three Peaks. Not so rugged as Penyghent and Ingleborough, it can be climbed from Ribblehead or from Ingleton. Near the summit are the tarns on which black-headed gulls breed. From Ribblehead, the distance to the top is three miles. Cross under the viaduct to Winterscale Farm, following the stream onto the open moor.

Ling Gill Nature Reserve. Noted for its rich limestone vegetation, this small valley off the Ribble is best approached

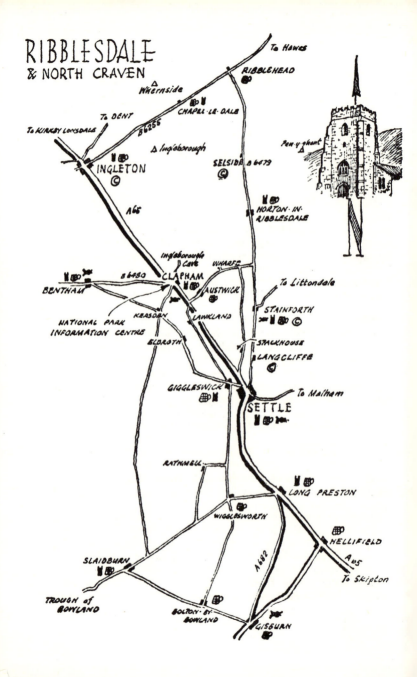

RIBBLESDALE
& NORTH CRAVEN

To Hawes

RIBBLEHEAD

△ Whernside

CHAPEL·LE·DALE

To Dent

B6255

To KIRKBY LONSDALE

△ Ingleborough

SELSIDE B6479

Pen·y·ghent

INGLETON

A65

HORTON·IN·RIBBLESDALE

Ingleborough Cave

WHARFE

B6480

CLAPHAM

To Littondale

BENTHAM

AUSTWICK

STAINFORTH

NATIONAL PARK
INFORMATION CENTRE

KEASDEN

LAWKLAND

STACKHOUSE

ELDROTH

LANGCLIFFE

GIGGLESWICK

To Malham

SETTLE

RATHMELL

LONG PRESTON

WIGGLESWORTH

HELLIFIELD

A65

SLAIDBURN

A682

To Skipton

TROUGH of
BOWLAND

BOLTON·BY·BOWLAND

GISBURN

from High Birkwith Farm, on a lane from Horton-in-Ribblesdale. It lies on the east side of the dale from Selside. There are some deep limestone shafts known as the Calf Holes. Colt Park reserve, near Selside, is open with permission from Nature Conservancy Council, 33 Eskdale Terrace, Newcastle upon Tyne.

Selside. 2½m Ribblehead, B6479. A group of old farmhouses, once owned by Furness Abbey, it now boasts a caravan site. It is the nearest place to:

Alum Pot (The Mouth of Hell). This is reached by a lane from the main road above the hamlet. It is 292 feet deep and is shielded by a clump of trees. The pothole is 130 feet long. No attempt should be made to enter without proper equipment and professional organisation.

Newhouses. A small collection of farm buildings near Horton, on the lane to High Birkwith. Tarn Dub, near the river, is the water from Alum Pot.

Hull Pot. On the flank of Penyghent, this great gash is 60 feet deep and 300 feet long, with a stream splashing through it. The pothole is reached by the green lane next to Horton Vicarage. As this comes to the open moor, the pot lies straight in front. A Pennine Way sign is at the green lane junction with the main road.

Penyghent. Likened to a crouching lion, the hill has deep waterworn scars on its flanks. The true summit, 2,273 feet high, is the cairn at the southern end, overlooking Horton. Care should be taken, particularly if mist forms. The shortest ascent is by the green lane from the Vicarage to the moor near Hull Pot (5m).

Horton-in-Ribblesdale. B6479, 6m from Settle. Although disfigured somewhat by limestone quarries, Horton has many attractions, particularly for the walker and potholer. Behind it rears the 'crouching lion' mass of Penyghent. There are old stone houses and bridges, and a fine old church with a massive stone tower. Dedicated to St. Oswald, it has a fragment of stained glass in one window which is probably a picture of the head of Thomas a Becket. The Pennine Way passes through the village and climbs Penyghent. Horton is an important point in the annual Three Peaks Race. The Settle-Carlisle railway is close to the village, but the station is closed for passengers. There is a limited bus service to Settle.

Inn: The Crown.
Shops: Post Office. Garage.
Cafe: Three Peaks. Car Park and Toilets.
Camping Site: Holme Farm, tents.

The road runs down the dale to Helwith Bridge (Hotel), where a turn off right leads to Austwick, and climbs Sherriff Brow, with fine views of the river gorge, to reach:

Stainforth. B6479, 2m from Settle. A pleasant village, once on an important packhorse route, its houses cluster round a beck and a small church. Crossing Cowside Beck by stepping stones, a walk of a mile or so up a steep green lane gives access to Catrigg Foss, a splendid waterfall (the paths are steep and are slippery after rain). A steep lane (Goat Lane) climbs from the head of the village to Malham Moor and Halton Gill.

Just above the village, a road crosses the railway and drops down Dog Hill to Stainforth Bridge, an old and picturesque packhorse bridge (built 1670s) on the road to Little Stainforth, or Knight Stainforth. Below the bridge is Stainforth Foss. Knight Stainforth Hall has some walled-up windows, a sequel to the window tax. The road from Little Stainforth continues on the far bank of the river through Stackhouse into Giggleswick. There is a pleasant riverside walk to Settle from Stainforth Bridge.

Inn: The Craven Heifer.
Post Office. Garage. Youth Hostel.
Caravan Site at Little Stainforth, T.
Limited bus service to Settle.

Langcliffe. B6479, 1m from Settle. Lying off the main road, the village has a pleasant green, from which a very steep lane leads to Malham Moor and then to Littondale. Langcliffe Hall is 17th century.

Caravan Site, T. Picnic area.
Limited bus service to Settle.

A cart track from the top of Langcliffe Brow leads to:

Victoria Cave, a famous 'bone' cave discovered in 1938. Remains of Iron Age man and animals were found (1m).

Stackhouse. Across the river from Langcliffe, this small hamlet has a hall which had connections with Furness Abbey. John Carr, the founder of Giggleswick School, lived there.

SETTLE

The capital of North Ribblesdale, Settle has many fine old buildings grouped round a market place, with a frowning limestone crag overlooking it. This is called 'Castleberg' and is open to the public, giving wide views. An Anglican settlement, Settle was originally in the parish of Giggleswick until the parish church was built in 1838. The Town Hall, used by the Rural District Council until the boundary changes in April 1974, was built in 1832 on the site of the old toll booth. The river bridge is medieval; salmon come up the river to the weir above the bridge.

The row of shops on the top side of the market, called The Shambles, was originally butchers' shops. There is a row of fine 18th century buildings in Cheapside next to the Town Hall. Behind this is High Street, leading to the old road to Long Preston, with a splendid house called The Folly. Built in the 17th century by the Preston family it was never completed. A cafe in the Market Place was once an inn called the Naked Man and has a stone effigy with the date in a strategic position.

The church, near the railway viaduct, has a marble plaque commemorating the many workmen who lost their lives in the district when the railway was built between 1869 and 1876.

There are several shops, banks, cafes and inns, and two car parks as well as the Market Place. Pennine buses link with Skipton and Ingleton. Rail links with Leeds and Carlisle or, at Giggleswick (1m), with Morecambe.

Population: **2,300.**
Market Day: Tuesday. Early Closing Day: Wednesday.
Tourist Information Centre: Town Hall (tel. 3617).
Swimming Pool. Golf Course at Giggleswick. Bowls.
Drama Festival: May.
Inn: Falcon. Golden Lion. Royal Oak.
Several garages.

Giggleswick. Off A65, ½m from Settle. The main road, after crossing Settle bridge, skirts the village, which lies down a hill to the left grouped round a stream called the river Tems. The church of St. Alkelda has a lych gate, and the old market cross near to it. Stained glass depicts the saint baptising converts. There is a bucket at the font which was used to carry water from the remarkable ebbing and flowing well under Giggleswick Scar, a short distance up Buckhaw Brow on the **A65.**

There are several fine old cottages in the village, but the largest group of buildings is Giggleswick School, founded in 1507. The splendid domed chapel on the hill behind the school was built to commemorate Queen Victoria's Jubilee by a wealthy governor, Walter Morrison of Malham Tarn House. The dome is of copper. Permission to visit should be sought from the lodge near the road.

Buckhaw Brow, which climbs under the Scar, gives wide views at the summit.

Inns: Black Horse, Harts Head. Craven Arms (at the railway station, 1m).
Shops. Golf Course. Garages in Settle.
Rail: Leeds to Morecambe line.
Buses: Pennine, Skipton-Ingleton.

Rathmell. 2½m from Settle and Giggleswick. A pleasant farming community, with a church, a chapel and an inn. A local man, Richard Frankland, established the first non-conformist college in England.

Bus to Settle (Tuesdays only).

Wigglesworth. B6478, 1m from Long Preston. Another small village, once the seat of the influential landowners, the Hammertons, whose home, the hall, is now two farms. There is an interesting building, the Plough Inn. A road climbs over moorland to the Forest of Bowland.

Bus to Settle (Tuesdays only).

Long Preston. A65, 3½m from Settle. A long straggling village, with a fine, tree-shaded green, it has an old parish church just off the main road in a quiet corner. On the Gisburn road (A682) are the almshouses, founded in 1613 by James Knowle, a local merchant who made a fortune in London.

Inns: Maypole. Boar's Head.
Garage.
Caravan Site: Crow Trees, Tosside, T, MC.
Rail: Leeds-Morecambe line.
Buses: Pennine, Skipton-Ingleton.

Hellifield. A65, 6m from Settle. Enlarged by the development of the railway around 1880, the older part of the village lies off the A65, on the road which joins the A682. Hellifield Peel, a three-storey fortified tower, was built by the Hammerton family in the reign of Henry VI. It is now in ruins. Near the village on the Gisburn road is a fine old house, now a farm. Called Arnford, it was built in 1690. There is an important auction mart.

Shops.
Inn: The Black Horse.
Rail: Leeds-Morecambe line.
Buses: Pennine, Skipton-Ingleton.

About 4 miles down the A682 is the hamlet of Newsholme, and a road off to the right to Paythorne Bridge. On this medieval structure, people gather in November to watch the salmon on 'Salmon Sunday.'

Gisburn. Junction of A682 and A59. Gisburn Hall and its fine park was the home of the Lords Ribblesdale. The main road is busy with traffic, and there are several cafes and an important auction mart. The Ribblesdale Arms, an imposing building, is dated 1635.

Garage.
Caravan Sites: Little Todber Caravan Park (on A59), MC.
Buses: Skipton-Clitheroe (Ribble).

Gisburn is a good point to enter the Forest of Bowland, designated as an Area of Outstanding Natural Beauty. Villages such as Slaidburn, Bolton-by-Bowland and Dunsop Bridge are worth visiting. Roads through Bowland lead to Clapham, Bentham or Lancaster. The river Hodder runs through the area with Stocks reservoir in the middle region.

Leaving the Ribble valley, the A65 runs north-west past the group of villages dominated by Ingleborough, the best known of the Three Peaks. Eldroth, Lawkland and Keasden are all small communities, linked by roads from Clapham and Giggleswick. Lawkland has a fine old hall. Keasden, a scattered community, lies on the road from Clapham which climbs high over Bowland Knotts into Slaidburn.

Austwick. Turn right off A65 at Cross Streets Inn, ½m (4½m from Settle). Minor road links with Horton-in-Ribblesdale. Comprising old houses grouped round patches of green, Austwick is ringed by three hills—Norber (with interesting weather-worn boulders on summit), Moughton and Oxenber. The church was once a chapel of ease to Clapham. The hall dates from 1189. From the road out of the top of the village, an old green road leads to Clapham, with fine views of Ingleborough. There is also a footpath from near the church over the fields to Clapham. The tiny hamlet of Wharfe lies under Moughton. The area is rich in wild flowers, and is popular with botanists and geologists.

Inns: The Game Cock. Cross Streets Hotel (1m on A65). The Traddock Guest House.

Garage. Shops and Post Office.

Buses to Ingleton, Settle and Skipton.

Clapham. Off A65, 6m from Settle. By-passed by the main road, Clapham lies on its own beck, with many trees and a waterfall near the church at the top of the village. The church tower is Norman, but the rest was enlarged by the Farrer family, who are still lords of the manor, in the 19th century. Their original home, Ingleborough Hall, is now an outdoor centre for North Yorkshire schools. The old manor house is now a National Park Information Centre, with car park adjoining.

Just above the village is the lake, built by the Farrers in 1828, and filled by the stream which flows off Ingleborough through the huge pothole of Gaping Gill (364 feet deep). There are descents of the pothole by winch in May and in August. One mile from the village, above the lake, is Ingleborough Cavern, a show cave open (daily in the summer) to the public. It is reached by a path through the estate grounds, entered by Saw Mill Cottage at the top of the village. There is a Nature Trail here. A footpath continues above the cave through Trow Gill, a limestone gorge to Gaping Gill, and to the summit of Ingleborough.

Inns: The New Inn. The Flying Horseshoe (1m at Clapham station). Goat Gap Farm (1½m), licensed restaurant.
Garage. Shops and Post Office.
Art Group Exhibition: May.
Caravans: Flying Horseshoe (near station).
Cave Rescue Centre: National Park Information Centre (next to car park).
Buses to Ingleton, Settle and Skipton.
Railway to Skipton, Leeds and Lancaster.

Newby. Part of the Clapham parish, the village lies off the main road grouped round a green. Newby Hall is 17th century. There was a grange here in monastic times.

Ingleborough (2,373 feet). The best known of the Three Peaks has a flat top and remains of a Brigantean fortress. It was used as a Roman signal station. The flanks contain many potholes. The ascent is normally from Clapham or Ingleton. Although of limestone generally, the mountain has a gritstone cap.

Ingleton. On A65. The old village lies at the foot of Ingleborough, to the north of the main road. The church of St. Mary is prominent, overlooking the valley which is crossed by a now disused railway viaduct. The two rivers, Twiss and Doe, have formed glens which are spectacular with waterfalls and rapids. Footpaths in the glens are open to the public, with access from the road over the bridge (about 4½m walk). The limestone scenery around is regarded as some of the finest in England. About two miles up the B6255 road to Hawes is White Scar Cave, a show cave open to the public daily (electric light, car park).

From nearby Thornton in Lonsdale, a spectacular road through Kingsdale terminates in Dent dale. Though well surfaced, the road is narrow and steep. There are several well known potholes in this area. Yordas, which lies near the head of the valley, is 180 feet long.

The Chapel-le-Dale valley, extending from Ingleton between Whernside and Ingleborough, passes over Storrs Common, from which the footpath to Ingleborough summit commences. About three miles from Ingleton (B6255) is the hamlet of Chapel-le-Dale, with a tiny church of St. Leonard. In it a monument commemorates the men who died during the building of the Settle-Carlisle railway between 1869 and 1876. Hurtle Pot is behind the church, and Weathercote Cave a short distance upstream. The Hill Inn (c.1615), is a centre for the Three Peaks races.

The old high road runs from the top of Ingleton, passing an old coaching inn, Holly Platt (now a farm), and dropping into Clapham.

Several Shops. Cafes.

Early Closing Day: Thursday.

Inns: **Three Horseshoes. Craven Heifer. Mason's Arms. Ingleborough Hotel. Bridge Hotel.**

Caravan Sites: Skirwith Farms (Hawes road). Broadwood Caravans, MC. Three Peaks Cafe, T, MC. The Trees, Westhouse (A65), T, MC.

Youth Hostel. Angling.

Brochure from Ingleton Publicity Association.

Buses to Skipton, Settle, Kendal, Lancaster and Morecambe.

Thornton in Lonsdale. This small village, about a mile from Ingleton, lies at the foot of Kingsdale. There is a church, rebuilt after a fire in the 1930s, and an inn, The Marton Arms (16th century).

Bentham. B6480 from Clapham. High and Low Bentham lie on the river Wenning, which flows into the Lune and eventually the Irish Sea. Clapham and Austwick becks are the main sources of the Wenning. High Bentham is a farming centre, with a weekly auction and a market established in 1306. Crossing the Wenning to Green Smithy brings the tourist to splendid moorland, with wide views. The church at High Bentham was built in 1838, but the one at Low

Bentham is Norman. Lowgill, nearby, leads to Tatham Fells and fine moorland.

Buses: Ribble buses from Ingleton and Lancaster.
Several Inns. Shops. Post Office.
Market Day: Wednesday. Early Closing Day: Thursday.
Caravan Parks: Riverside Caravan Park, T.

BOOKS

Around Ingleton and Clapham.

Bowland and Pendle Hill.

Settle-Carlisle Railway.

Settle and North Craven.

(All Dalesman Publishing Company.)

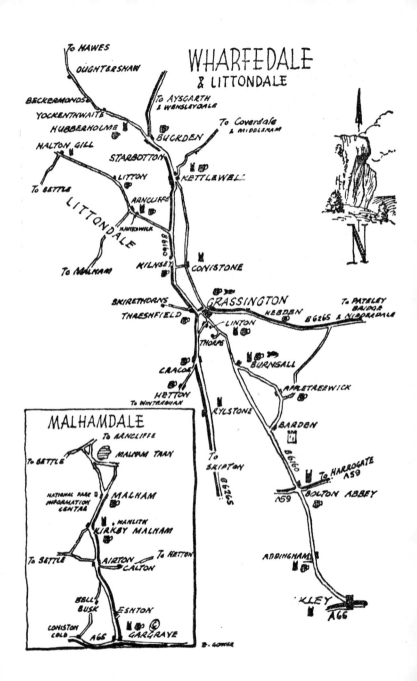

Malhamdale and Wharfedale

MALHAMDALE

A SHORT valley from which the river Aire flows, Malhamdale has some of the most impressive scenery in the National Park and is very popular with tourists, school, botany and geology parties, walkers and climbers. The road to it from Gargrave (A65) is narrow. The exit roads at the head of the dale, to Settle or Littondale, are also narrow and very steep.

Gargrave. On the A65, this is a big village astride the Aire with several shops and inns. Not actually in Malhamdale, it is the entry for many people. Two miles from Gargrave, going north, at Coniston Cold, another road enters the dale via Bell Busk and Airton. The Leeds and Liverpool Canal passes through the village, with holiday cruises available. There is a caravan site at Gargrave on the Eshton road (T, MC), and another at the Anchor Inn, next to the canal locks.

Eshton. A large house set in parkland, Eshton Hall is now a nursing home. It was built by the influential Wilson family. Sir Matthew Wilson was Skipton's first M.P. in 1885.

Just before the hall, a road branches right to Flasby, a hamlet, and on to Hetton and Grassington. Past the hall, another right fork leads to Winterburn, passing a fine old farmhouse called Friars Head. Shortly afterwards is Newfield Hall, a guest house.

Airton. Lacking both church and inn, this stone built village has a green with a 'squatter's' cottage in the middle. The old mill, which goes back to the Canons of Bolton Priory, stands next to the river and has been converted into apartments. Just above it is a group of 18th century houses built by Quakers; the Meeting House is still used. The school on the green is closed. There is a footpath (Pennine Way) on the riverside to Malham.

Crossing the river and up a steep bend, the road goes to the hamlet of Calton, which has some fine old houses. Calton Hall is on the site of a previous house in which lived General Lambert, who became one of Cromwell's chief officers and suffered exile at the hands of Charles II after the Stuart restoration. The road turns sharp right to Winterburn and Grassington.

Scotsthrop adjoins Airton where the road turns off to Settle. A hamlet of old farms, the name comes from the Scottish settlers in the 11th century. The manor house on the right is 17th century. A footpath leaves the road near here to join the riverside path.

Petrol Station.

Kirkby Malham. A small and charming village dominated by the church of St. Michael, which has a pre-Danish foundation and was rebuilt in the 15th century, this collection of old houses and farms used to have a bobbin mill supplying wooden bobbins for Lancashire cotton mills. The imposing vicarage, next to the church, was the old hall, built in 1622 but modernised in the 19th century. It has been used as a workhouse and a cotton mill. The inn at bridge end was used by churchwardens for both drinking and selling ale. The old stocks are inside the churchyard.

A short distance towards Malham, at Cockthorns Hill, are terraced fields called 'lychets,' used in Anglian days when the common fields were ploughed. The joint school for Kirkby and Malham lies between the two villages.

Inn: The Victoria.

Malham. At an elevation of 650 feet, this ancient village is overshadowed by massive limestone fells. The beck divides Malham East and West — East belonged to Bolton Priory and West to Fountains Abbey. There are several 17th century buildings, narrow winding lanes and four bridges. The main bridge, originally called Monk Bridge (the monks built it), is in two sections of different ages. What is left of the old hall is now the reading room, to the left of the bridge. The

Lister Arms Inn is an old building with varying date stones — one, on an outbuilding, is 1702. A short distance up the Cove road is Cromwell Cottage, and a clapper bridge (Moon Bridge) leading to Beck Hall, an ancient house.

Modern Youth Hostel in the village.

Behind the Methodist chapel is a large car park, and the National Park Information Centre (tel. Airton 363).

Malham Show: August.

Inns: The Buck. The Lister Arms. Cafe and Shop.

Pennine bus from Skipton serving all the villages in Malhamdale.

Malham Cove. A huge limestone cliff about ½m from the village, the Cove is visible on approaching from Kirkby Malham. A gate and stile lead off the Cove road, which is steep and narrow with parking prohibited, and the footpath goes across the field near the beck. Just below the stile is the site of Malham Mill, originally a cornmill, which was used later as a cotton mill and pulled down in the late 19th century. The little waterfall near the site is called Old Mill Foss. The limestone cliff, The Cove, is 240 feet high and at one time water fell over it. The stream that burbles from it comes from the moor above, where it sinks into the ground near the old smelt mill. A steep footpath climbs to the left to the limestone pavements at the top, where the deep waterworn crevices can be crossed with care. It is dangerous to go near the edge, as the limestone is liable to break off. The dry valley behind the Cove is where the water used to flow to make the waterfall.

Gordale Scar and Janet's Foss. From the green in the centre of Malham, Finkle Street runs by the side of the cafe. A short distance on this lane is the ruin of Friar Garth, and opposite it is the steep road to Malham Tarn. About a mile from the village the Gordale road drops and twists, and opposite a barn is a footpath to the right giving access to Janet's Foss. This is a miniature cove, with a waterfall dropping into a deep pool, which is said to be the haunt of a fairy called Janet. Below the fall a footpath follows the stream back to Friar Garth.

Returning to the road and crossing the new bridge, with the far more attractive old one alongside, Gordale Scar can be seen to the left. There is a footpath by the farm. The great gorge, 400 feet high, has a waterfall splashing down it. This can be climbed by the agile, and a footpath leads to the Malham Tarn road.

Malham Tarn. The road diverging at Malham from the one to Gordale climbs up to the Tarn, and the road past the cove which joins another on the moor top also passes close to it. The Tarn is half a mile in diameter. Its fishing rights belonged to Fountains Abbey. Tarn House was originally an old shooting lodge of the Listers, but Walter Morrison rebuilt it in 1850. Charles Kingsley stayed here when writing *The Water Babies*. It is now National Trust property and a Field Centre; there was a tower on the building until a few years ago. The water from the Tarn sinks underground and reappears at Aire Head Springs below Malham village. Below this point, together with other becks, it forms the river Aire.

Angling: Boat only. Apply 10 days in advance to the Warden, Malham Tarn Field Centre (tel. Airton 331).

The roads out of Malham are steep and narrow, and not suitable for coaches. It is best to leave vehicles in the large car park at the entrance to the village from Kirkby Malham. The area has many footpaths and is splendid walking country. From Malham Tarn, roads run to Settle and to Arncliffe in Littondale. The old green road, Mastiles Lane, crosses the moor to Kilnsey in Wharfedale, with a branch to Threshfield via Bordley. To the east of the Tarn, above the scar, is Great Close. This was the scene of the Malham Moor cattle fairs; in the 18th century, 5,000 Scotch cattle would be gathered here. The moor is rich in prehistoric remains, with traces of Iron Age hutments, Bronze Age relics and flint implements. The stone walls, which climb over the fells and enclose the fields round the village, were built in the 18th century when the common field agriculture was gradually abandoned. There are no caravan or camping sites on Malham Moor.

BOOKS

Malham (Dalesman).

Malham and Malham Moor, Arthur Raistrick (Dalesman).

WHARFEDALE

UPPER WHARFEDALE, that is the area north of Ilkley, is one of the most popular of the larger dales. It is largely limestone country, with fine river scenery, high moors and fells, and several villages providing for the tourist and holidaymaker. The northern part is narrow and wild, with high passes linking with Wensleydale and Coverdale. Littondale, which runs off north-west from just above the spectacular Crag at Kilnsey, has high roads connecting with Malhamdale and Settle. Ilkley is the only town. This moorland spa has good links with the rest of the country, including rail, bus and the Leeds-Bradford Airport at Yeadon. Grassington, a large village with good shops and tourist accommodation, is the centre of the upper dale. Skipton, the ancient market town of the dale, is closely connected with the area. Wharfedale offers a ruined abbey, waterfalls, rapids, ancient churches, unspoilt villages, potholes and some of the finest walking and touring country in England.

ILKLEY

The Romans had a station here called 'Olicana,' and in the 19th century the natural springs attracted people in search of cures. The town developed into an inland resort, with pleasant tree-lined streets, gardens, river attractions, and the famour moor. Hotels and shops were built, and the good communications brought prosperity to the town. Many wealthy business people from the West Riding towns came to live here, and built good houses. There is a theatre, a public library, sports facilities, and a museum near the church in the restored Elizabethan Manor House.

The Cow and Calf Rocks on the moor above the town are an attraction, and there are Bronze and Iron Age carved stones, also on the moor, which has many footpaths and a charming little tarn. The church has three Runic crosses in the churchyard, and the remains of Roman altars built into the base of the tower.

Population: 19,000.
Early Closing Day: Wednesday.
Good shops, hotels, cafes, garages, etc.
Swimming pool, boating, tennis, etc.
Angling: Day permits from Crees Pet Stores, Leeds Road, Ilkley.
Buses to Skipton, Harrogate, Bradford, Leeds.

Addingham. A65, 3m from Ilkley. A long cluster of stone houses, this large village has a main road running through a narrow street. There is much history in the place and there are several old houses—some, of three storeys, were once used for domestic weaving. It has a church, shops, banks, etc., and buses from Ilkley, Skipton and Keighley pass through.

Inns, Garages.
Caravan Parks: The Paddocks Caravan Site, Bolton Abbey Road, T, MC. Olicana Caravan Park, High Mill, T, MC.
Buses from Ilkley, Skipton and Keighley.

Bolton Bridge (14th century). The A65 from Addingham crosses the A59 Skipton to Harrogate road here. Not far up the Harrogate road is Beamsley 'hospital' built in 1593 by the mother of Lady Anne Clifford, of Skipton Castle, for old ladies. The unusual circular chapel building and cottages may be visited. From the bridge, the road up the dale runs past the Devonshire Arms Hotel, and soon passes a splendid large tithe barn on the right to enter:

Bolton Abbey village. B6160. The village of Bolton is much older than the famous ruin, which is not an abbey but a priory. Of Anglican origins, the area became the property of a Norman, Robert Romille, who later moved to Skipton and built the castle there.

Car parks in the village. Post Office. Cafe.
Buses from Skipton and Ilkley.
Caravans: The Strid Wood, T.

Bolton Priory. B6160. Parts of the precinct wall are alongside the road, and 'The Hole in the Wall' gives access to the priory grounds. A short distance on the road is Bolton Hall, the shooting lodge of the Duke of Devonshire which was built in the 1850s on the site of the old gatehouse. Near this a narrow arch which restricts speed is an 18th century aqueduct.

The views from the 'hole' over the level, riverside meadow, with the priory ruins, the rectory, the stepping stones and a footbridge under a high cliff, are splendid. Beyond the river the hills rise to Simon Seat. There are hollows which were the priory's fishponds, and the rectory, built about 1700, includes part of the infirmary. The extensive ruins of the priory include a cloister, frater, chapter house, prior's lodging, and the church, which continued in use after the Dissolution. The present day church is only the nave of the original, but contains much of historic interest. The priory is open daily.

Bolton Woods and the Strid. For two miles or so above the priory, the Wharfe passes through lovely scenery. At the Cavendish Pavilion (refreshments) a toll bridge gives access to the opposite bank, or the path can be followed for a mile to the Strid. This narrow gorge has been the scene of drownings and it is unwise to try to jump across. There is also access to the Strid from the dale road nearer Barden. Road access to Cavendish Pavilion and car park is from the

Cavendish Memorial. There is a Nature Trail.

Angling: Tickets from the Estate Offices.

Barden Tower. B6160. About two miles from Bolton Abbey, the ruined Barden Tower stands to the right. Enlarged from a forest lodge by Henry Lord Clifford of Skipton Castle in the 15th century, the tower was repaired in 1657 by Lady Anne Clifford, but became ruinous after 1774. There is a chapel and an attendant's house. It is possible to see this tower from the outside only. Just past this, a right fork leads to Barden Bridge, a graceful arched 17th century structure. Masons' marks can be seen on the stones. A footpath from here gives entry to the woods and leads downstream to the Strid. There is a small charge.

The old school across from the tower is used by the National Park Warden Service. From Barden Bridge the road follows the river through the hamlet of Howgill, nestling under Simon Seat with its prominent rocks, to the attractive village of:

Appletreewick. Straggling on each side of the street, the village has several old houses. Monks Hall is on the site of property belonging to Bolton Priory; the pigeon holes and outside stairs are late 17th century. High Hall, at the top of the street, was the home of the Craven family, of which Sir William, born in 1548, is the best known as he became Lord Mayor of London in 1610. The village was once well known for its Onion Fair. There are pleasant riverside walks.

Inns: Craven Arms. New Inn.

Buses: Limited bus service to Ilkley and Grassington.

Caravan Site and Camping Site near river.

Caravan Site at Howgill Lodge; also Howarth Farm, Skyreholme, T, MC; Cow Hall, T.

At the road junction before Appletreewick, a right turn leads to Skyreholme. A scattered hamlet, it has a disused paper mill which once had a large water wheel. Upstream is Trollers Gill, a limestone gorge, and across on a hill spur is Percival Hall, a restored Elizabethan house now used as a retreat by the Church of England. It is reputed to have been used by the highwayman William Nevison, from whom many of the Dick Turpin legends have sprung. The gardens are open to the public daily (May to September). Updale the road from Appletreewick passes through Hartlington. At the junction where the road turns off to Hebden there is an ancient farm, Summersgill. This is an example of the old dales 'Longhouse,' with the barn for the animals forming part of the house structure. It has been restored.

Burnsall. B6160. A popular village, with a green and a splendid river bridge, Burnsall has some houses of great antiquity near the church, which dates from the 12th century. Inside the church is a Norse-Danish font, and parts of Anglican crosses. The village stocks are in the churchyard, which is reached through a lychgate, operated by a system of weights. Next to the church is the fine Elizabethan school and master's house. Still in daily use and with little of its frontage altered, the school was founded in 1605 by William Craven of Appletreewick for boys in the parish. As this covered a large area, provision was made for the boys to board. The upper storey was divided into dormitory chambers by oak planks, and this structure is still there.

Inns: The Red Lion. The Fell Hotel.
Cafe. Petrol.
Car park on riverside. Toilets. Boating.
Burnsall Sports and Fell Race: Mid-August.
Limited bus service to Ilkley and Grassington.

Thorpe. A secluded village in the Burnsall parish, Thorpe is reached by a narrow lane from the B6160. A group of old houses and farms, under a rounded hill called Elbolton, the village is said to have had many cobblers making shoes for Fountains Abbey although experts think this unlikely. There is neither inn nor shop. There is a footpath from Burnsall and Linton.

Hebden. 2m from Grassington on B6265. The old bridge spans Hebden Beck, which flows down to join the Wharfe next to a suspension bridge. Crossing this, footpaths lead to Thorpe and Burnsall. The latter one, following the river, gives a good view of Loup Scar, a limestone gorge, near which are two ancient 'holy' wells, St. Helen's and St. Margaret's. Hebden has some 17th century houses, and the pleasant walk up the Gill passes Scale Force, a waterfall about halfway to Hole Bottom. From here a bridleway climbs to the moor, passing ruins of lead-mine workings, and leads to Yarnbury, where the road descends into Grassington. The village school celebrated its centenary in 1975. Near the school a footpath leads down to the beck and old mill dams, coming out at Hebden Mill (now cottages), from where a road leads to Burnsall.

Inn: Clarendon.
Shop and Post Office.
Caravan Site: Hebden Hall, Mill Lane.
Buses: Limited bus service to Grassington and Skipton; also to Pateley Bridge and Harrogate (summer weekends).

Linton. Reached from the Burnsall road at Great Bank Top crossroads, Linton has several old houses round a green, at one side of which is the beck. This is crossed by the road bridge (1892) which replaced two fords, and a short distance upstream by the packhorse bridge, called Redmayne Bridge, from the lady who repaired it in the 17th century. Higher up still is an ancient packhorse bridge, whose stone flags have been covered with tarmac. Near this is the imposing Fountaine Hospital, built in 1721 and containing six small houses and a chapel. It was designed by Vanbrugh, the architect of Castle Howard. Near the main road bridge is the Old Hall, a fine 17th century farm, with some equally impressive old barns up the road. Linton means 'flax' farm, and there was a flax industry here for centuries.

Buses: West Yorkshire from Skipton and Grassington.
Inn: The Fountaine.
Post Office and Shop. Youth Hostel in the old Rectory.

A footpath from the main bridge on the beckside leads to Threshfield. Another one, from the top of the village, at Grange Farm, goes to Thorpe.

Linton Church, Falls and Tin Bridge. The ancient church which serves the parish of Linton, Grassington, Threshfield and Hebden, lies next to the river about a mile from the village. It has no tower, but some 12th century Norman arches. Stepping stones from the field adjoining the churchyard form the old way for worshippers from Hebden. Opposite the church is Grassington Low Mill, recently converted into a dwelling. At the junction of the beck here, there was a lead smelting mill. There is a car park and toilets a few hundred yards from the church, near Botany, a hamlet built to house mill workers about 1850. The mill next to these, which is a modern structure on a very old mill site, has been closed since 1959. The manorial corn mill was here, and was later converted to textiles. A footpath goes behind the hedge at the end of the mill and leads to a quaint 14th century stone bridge, called by Halliwell Sutcliffe, the writer who lived in Linton, 'Lile Emily's Bridge.' It was probably part of the old corpse route from Threshfield to the church. Captain Beck, flowing under the bridge, empties into the Wharfe just above Linton Falls where large steps of limestone make the river very spectacular after heavy rain. The footbridge, 'Tin Bridge,' joins the 'snake walk' up the hill to Grassington. There are footpaths on both sides of the river to Grassington bridge, and on one side downstream to Hebden and Burnsall.

Between Linton Mill and Grassington bridge is Threshfield Free Grammar School, founded in 1674 by Matthew Hewitt, a rector of Linton. The fine building provided two rooms in the upper storey for the schoolmaster. Now controlled by the North Yorkshire County Council, the school has all modern facilities and is in regular use by local children. It is said to be haunted by 'Pam the Fiddler,' a musical ghost who pestered the schoolmaster.

The road from Linton to Skipton passes Catchall, a farm which was once an inn, and joins the road from Threshfield. A new straight stretch skirts the limestone works, and passes through:

Cracoe. B6265. A very narrow lane with no passing places turns off the main road at the quarry end of the village to Thorpe. Near the junction is **Threapland;** at the farm there is a camping site. Cracoe is pronounced 'Crayco.' Pleasant houses are on each side of the main road, but the old Skipton road, now a grassy track, runs behind the village and makes a pleasant walk. Cracoe Fell, rising behind, has an obelisk commemorating the men who died in the two wars and is a prominent landmark.

Inn: The Devonshire.
Post Office. Butcher's shop.
Buses: West Yorkshire, Skipton-Grassington.
Caravans: Threaplands, T.

Hetton. A road forks from the main road below Cracoe, crossing the old Yorkshire Dales Railway which ran from Skipton to Grassington. It is used now for quarry traffic only as far as Swinden Limeworks. A collection of old houses on the hillside, the village is colourful at times when the Pendle Forest Craven Harriers meet at the Angel Inn. The road continues to Gargrave, with one to the right leading to Winterburn and Airton.

Inns: The Angel.
Buses: West Yorkshire, Skipton-Grassington.

Rylstone. B6265. A small village grouped round a duck pond which was once the village green, Rylstone was the home of the Norton family, involved in the Pilgrimage of Grace. The ruins of their summer house, Norton Tower, can be seen on Rylstone Fell, whose craggy outline rears above the village. North-east of the tower is Rylstone Cross, commemorating the Battle of Waterloo. The church is a relatively modern building on the site of an early chapel-of-ease in the parish of Burnsall. Behind the church there are traces of the manor house of the Norton family. It was Kit Norton who tried to rescue Mary Queen of Scots from Bolton Castle. A minor road leads to Hetton.

Buses: West Yorkshire, Skipton-Grassington.

Threshfield. B6265. Standing at the junction of the updale road and that to Grassington, Threshfield really begins at the massive bridge over the beck. The house before the bridge with a cobbled pavement was the home of the famous besom makers, the Ibbottsons. Up the hill, old houses are grouped round the green with its tall trees, and facing the green is the Old Hall Inn which stands on the site of Threshfield Hall. On the other side of the green is the Manor House. Although mainly rebuilt, the porch and rose window are splendid parts of the original. The road from Burnsall, B6160, comes in at the back of the village behind the incongruous silo tower.

Inns: The Old Hall. Wilson Arms Hotel.
Petrol.
Caravan Site and Restaurant: Long Ashes (B6265), T.
Buses: West Yorkshire, Skipton-Grassington.

Skirethorns. A short distance updale from Threshfield a road turns off left, and in about half a mile reaches the hamlet of Skirethorns. There is a tiny green, with a stream, and a group of old farmhouses. The road above the village climbs to Malham, but is prohibited to vehicles after two miles.

Caravan Site: Wood Nook.

GRASSINGTON

B6265, 9½m from Skipton, 15m from Ilkley. The capital of the upper dale, Grassington is a big and busy village with shops, inns and quaint corners. The Square is cobbled and the fine Georgian Grassington House faces another old building, now Church House but originally a farm dwelling built in 1694. The village, of Anglian origins, seems to have been important long before the Normans, and, with roads from Nidderdale, Skipton and Wensleydale converging on it, became the centre of the area. The development of the lead-mines on Grassington Moor added to its population, and the adaptation of the old corn mills to textiles brought workers into the village. There was a decline about 1900, but the opening of the Yorkshire Dales Railway in 1901 brought people from the West Riding towns, developing the tourist trade and the limestone quarries. The population was restored to its 19th century level of around 1,100, a figure maintained today.

The Old Hall, hidden away behind the Devonshire Hotel, is probably the oldest house in the village, but there are several dated headstones to be seen in the Folds which run off the main street. At the top of Garrs Lane, running from the top right corner of the Square, is the Congregational chapel built in 1812. On the other side of the lane are some cottages on the site of the old theatre, founded by Tom Airey, who achieved some local fame as actor and manager. Behind these is a fine barn, often known as 'Wesley Barn' because John Wesley is reputed to have preached in it. The massive walls are pierced with arched ventilation slits and there is a pigeon cote. At the top of the main street is the Devonshire Institute, often called the Town Hall, and opposite to it is Chamber End Fold or King Street, with several 19th century lead-miners' cottages. The end house is 17th century.

On Chapel Street is Chapel Fold or Ranters Fold, where an old barn is now the workshop of a furniture craftsman, and at the far end is Town Head Farm with mullioned windows. This property belongs to the trustees of the Fountaine Hospital in Linton. A footpath through the yard runs over the fells to Conistone. Straight up from the Main Street is Moor Road. This climbs to Yarnbury, where a large house recently renovated was the residence of the manager of the lead-mines. Beyond this is the Moor and, on the far side of the gill which drops to Hebden, the old smelt mill chimney.

The Grassington and Upper Wharfedale Museum is in the Square. At the bottom of the Square, the roads runs east to Hebden and Pateley Bridge, while an updale road, Wood Lane, runs above the river and through Grass Woods to Conistone. Grass Woods is a Nature Reserve and is rich in wild flowers. It has many footpaths, one of which leads to Fort Gregory, occupied by the Brigantes who opposed the occupying Romans.

Grassington bridge, between Grassington and Threshfield, is on the site of a ford, and in 1603 replaced a wooden structure. The bridge is in two sections, the older, humpbacked one being widened in the 18th century and the approaches raised. Footpaths from it follow the river upstream to Conistone and downstream to Linton Falls and Burnsall. Half a mile upstream is a fine stretch of rapids —the Ghaistrills Strid. The riverside walk passing through Grassington is part of the **Dales Way** from Ilkley to Windermere.

There are obvious traces of an Iron Age settlement on

the hillside above the village, reached by the footpath from Town Head, and there is a Bronze Age barrow in Lea Green, the huge pasture which lies above Grass Woods. At the far end of this is Dibb Scar, a limestone gorge, from which a footpath meanders to Conistone.

Inns: The Devonshire. The Black Horse. The Forester's Arms. Grassington House Hotel. Ashfield Hotel. Cafes.

Buses: West Yorkshire to Skipton, Ilkley and Buckden. Weekend summer services to Harrogate, Wensleydale and Swaledale.

Early Closing: Thursday.

Post Office, shops, banks, garages.

National Park Information and administration centre at Colvend (next to car park on Hebden Road).

Upper Wharfedale Fell Rescue headquarters.

Annual Exhibition of Dales Arts and Crafts in August.

Angling: Tickets from Grassington Post Office, or Devonshire Hotel.

The Parish Church is at Linton. There are two Nonconformist churches and a new, rather unusual Roman Catholic church across the river, towards Threshfield.

Kilnsey and Conistone. B6160. The massive limestone Kilnsey Crag close to the dale road is well known, and the difficult climb over its bulge has been featured on television. The village is small, grouped round an old grange of Fountains Abbey. It was a great sheep centre in monastic days, and the corn from the Abbey lands around was ground here. The flat fields in front of the Crag were the base of a lake, formed after the melting of the glacier which cut the face of the huge rock. There are still important sheep sales held here, and the annual show on the Summer Bank Holiday Tuesday brings big crowds. The race up the Crag attracts entries from a wide area. The steep green road running from the head of the village is Mastiles Lane, which goes over the tops to Malham Tarn.

Inn: The Tennants Arms.

Bus: West Yorkshire from Skipton.

Angling: Tickets from Tennants Arms.

Across the river bridge, which is very old, is Conistone, a cluster of houses and a church. Behind the village is a narrow limestone gorge, and a lane climbs up to the flanks of Great Whernside at Mossdale. Some of the houses are 17th century. The church is of Saxon foundation and has two massive round arches on the north side of the nave. The roads lead to Grassington and Kettlewell.

Post Office.

Half a mile above Kilnsey there is a road junction — the left road is to Littondale, and the main dale road is to Kettlewell. Across the valley can be seen a group of buildings with a Scandinavian style church; this is Scargill House, a Church of England centre. Under Knipe Wood, there is a fine view of Kettlewell village across the river with the great fells behind.

Kettlewell. B6160, 6m from Grassington. Of ancient origins and having thriving times in monastic days, Kettlewell belonged to the Nevilles of Middleham in 1605. It became Crown property until Charles I granted it to some London merchants who sold it to local people. The Manor is still governed by the Trust Lords who are elected from the Freeholders. Although many of the older houses have been altered, the bridge is splendid, and the beck from Cam Gill and Dowber Gill runs between the houses. The 1885 school, which is halfway to the next village, Starbotton, is unusual in that it is a 'Board School.' The church was rebuilt in the 19th century.

The steep and twisty road from the head to the village climbs Park Rash and goes over to Coverdale and Middleham. In Park Gill, at the foot of Park Rash, is Dow Cave, which can be explored for a short distance if care is taken. There are several fine walks in the area.

Inns: The Bluebell. The Racehorses. The King's Head.

Post Office and Shop. Garage. Youth Hostel.

Early Closing: Thursday.

Angling: Tickets from Tennants Arms Hotel, Kilnsey.

Bus: West Yorkshire from Skipton. Weekend summer service from Bradford through Upper Wharfedale to Wensleydale and Swaledale.

Caravans: Causeway Croft, T.

Starbotton. 2m from Kettlewell, B6160. The road up the dale is close to the river here. The hillsides are patterned with limestone walls, running from the level meadows on the valley floor to the tops of the fells. Isolated outbarns are dotted here and there. The village of Starbotton is all grey limestone, weathered and coloured with moss. The houses are mainly 17th century, although several have been modernised and are used as holiday homes. In 1686 a great flood swept away many of the dwellings. The green road behind the village climbs up the Knuckle Bone to the summit of Buckden Pike. There are many examples of Anglian 'lynchets,' or cultivation terraces, to be seen between Starbotton and Buckden.

Inn: Fox and Hounds.
Bus: West Yorkshire from Skipton.

Buckden. B6160, 10m from Grassington. A small village in an important position at the junction of two roads, Buckden derives its name from the deer that once lived in the area and was the residence of the officers of Langstrothdale forest. Buckden Pike (2,302 feet) is above the village. There are some old cottages, a car park and picnic area. The B6160 goes to Cray, and then over Kidstones Pass to Bishopdale and Aysgarth. The other road, to the left from the small green, leads into Langstrothdale and over Fleet Moss to Hawes in Wensleydale.

Inn: The Buck. Post Office and Shop.
Angling: Tickets from The Buck Inn.
Bus: Limited West Yorkshire service to Skipton (not Sundays).

Hubberholme. At Kirk Gill, 1m from Buckden, is the fine Hubberholme church, and across the bridge, the George Inn, once the vicarage. Even as an inn it belonged to the church and was kept by the churchwarden. The church was originally in the parish of Arncliffe, and the parson from there rode over the fell to take the service. The sexton at Hubberholme watched for his white horse and then rang the bell to call the congregation. The massive tower is 13th century, and there is a rare rood screen dating from 1558. The pews are by a modern craftsman, Thompson of Kilburn, known as the 'Mouseman.' On the church side of the river, a road joins that from Buckden in Cray Gill. At **Cray,** a tiny hamlet with some nearby waterfalls, is the White Lion Inn, where the antlers of the last deer to be killed in the valley are to be seen.

Yockenthwaite. Updale from Hubberholme the river flows through open land — a popular place for picnics. Before dropping to Yockenthwaite bridge the road passes the farm of Raisgill, behind which is the old green road, the Horse Head Pass, to Foxup in Littondale. Yockenthwaite, of Norse origins, is now a tiny hamlet, but there are records of other houses, an inn and a school. On the north side of the river, just beyond the houses, is a Bronze Age stone circle with twenty stones standing on edge. The river here has cut rock pools and little gorges in the limestone. There are few trees, and the dale is wild and beautiful. A little bridge crosses the river at Deepdale, where there is a group of old farmhouses. There is an Iron Age village on the west side of Deepdale Gill, about 1,600 feet up.

Oughtershaw. A mile or so further up the dale, Oughtershaw Beck joins the one from Greenfield to form the river Wharfe, and at the junction is the hamlet of Beckermonds. This was once the hunting forest of Langstrothdale, and at Greenfield, reached by a road from Beckermonds, there has been extensive tree planting. From Greenfield a green road continues round Birkwith Moor to Horton-in-Ribblesdale — this is an ancient packhorse route to Lancaster. The road to the right from the junction of the becks leads into Oughtershaw, which stands at 1,200 feet. The hall, in a deep gorge, is fairly modern, and the small school was built in 1847 by the Wood family, who lived in the hall. The road continues over Fleet Moss to Hawes, but the old track by the beck goes to Cam Houses, where it joins the Roman road from Bainbridge. The Fleet Moss road gives spectacular views, but it is steep in places and quickly affected by snow or mist.

LITTONDALE

The flat bottomed glacial valley, which was once called Amerdale, runs off to the north-west about half a mile above Kilnsey. The river in the dale is the Skirfare, which joins the Wharfe at Hammerdale Dub. The limestone fells climb steeply from the valley, and geology students will find plenty of interest. There is a road on either side — the one on the left runs straight to Arncliffe, the other passing through Hawkswick. Half a mile up the Arncliffe road, at Sleets Gill, there is a cave under the limestone scar, and a mile further up is Dowkerbottom Cave. These can be entered with care. Remains of prehistoric man and animals have been found here.

Hawkswick. The village has some old buildings near the river. A bridge leads across the dale to Hawkswick and Arncliffe Cotes, which were former granges of Fountains Abbey and are still sheep farms. There is a caravan site here (Hawkswick Cote, T, MC).

Arncliffe. This is the principal village in the dale. It clusters round a green, and has a fine old church next to the river. An old corn mill at the far end of the green has been converted into flats. Cowside Beck runs alongside it from Malham Moor, passing through a wild gorge, Yew Cogar Scar. The inn, the Falcon, was for many years the home of Marmaduke Miller, a well known Dales artist. The house at Bridge End, with a lawn running down to the river, was a favourite place of Charles Kingsley during the time he stayed at Malham Tarn and conceived *The Water Babies*. The church has been largely restored but the tower is Norman. Inside is a list of the Arncliffe men who fought at the Battle of Flodden in 1513. A steep, twisty and gated road from the village leads to Malham (10m), Langcliffe, and then to Settle. It passes the remote Darnbrook Farm in a steep little valley.

Inn: The Falcon. Amerdale House Hotel.
Post Office.

Litton. This small village gives its name to the dale. It is two miles from Arncliffe, and has some 17th century houses. A track climbs over to Hubberholme, and from the bridge, a short distance up river, a green road mounts the fell and joins the motor road from Halton Gill.

Inn: The Queen's Arms.
Post Office.

Halton Gill. Overshadowed by great fells, this hamlet of 17th century houses has a church and once had a school. Its population is less than it was in 1867 when the schoolmaster earned £10 a year. The school, now a cottage, was attached to the chapel which was rebuilt in 1636. It was the only school in Littondale for two hundred years, and closed in 1957. The road across the river climbs between Fountains Fell and Penyghent, over wild sheep country, into Stainforth, with the Ribblesdale road then going into Settle. Above Halton Gill is **Foxup,** where the road ends.

SKIPTON

The old market town has strong links with Wharfedale. The Honour of the town in feudal times had its origins in the estates centred on Bolton Abbey, belonging to the Saxon Earl Edwin. After Domesday the lands were granted to Robert de Romille, who is believed to have started building the castle. The Cliffords, whose name is now much associated with the town, came into possession in 1309.

The town has a wide High Street, with stalls on the edges several days in the week, and has good shops and several old inns. There are large free car parks. The canal has a developing traffic in holiday craft. There is an important cattle auction mart. The castle is open daily; the parish church next to it is of the 14th century. The Craven Museum is in the Town Hall. The High Corn Mill near the church houses a museum.

Market Days: Monday, Wednesday, Saturday.
Early Closing: Tuesday.
Population: 13,000.
Golf, Tennis, Swimming Pool, etc.
Buses to Leeds, Bradford, Ilkley, Otley, Grassington, Keighley (West Yorkshire); Settle, Ingleton (Pennine); Manchester and East Lancashire (Ribble).
ParkLink service (bus and train) from Leeds and Bradford to Skipton and Upper Wharfedale.
Trains to London, Glasgow, Leeds, Bradford, Morecambe.

Caravans: Tarn House Caravan Park (off B6265), T, MC. Over-dale Trailer Park, Harrogate Road (A59), T, MC.

Embsay. 2m from Skipton, Embsay is the headquarters of the Yorkshire Dales Railway Society. The display is open daily except Tuesday, and there are steam trains on Sundays and public holidays.

BOOKS

Grassington; A History of Grassington; The Dales Way; Walking in the Craven Dales; Wharfedale; Railways in the Yorkshire Dales.

(All Dalesman Publishing Company.)

Nidderdale

ALTHOUGH not in the Yorkshire Dales National Park, Nidderdale is just as attractive as the other dales and is less well known. The upper reaches are wild and remote, not being crossed by the high pass roads as are some neighbouring valleys. The reservoirs of Scar House and Angram, under the mass of Great Whernside, absorb the infant Nidd, and, lower down, Gouthwaite reservoir has the appearance of a natural lake. Below Pateley Bridge, the dale widens and mellows until the dramatic gorge at Knaresborough, and from there the Nidd crosses fertile plains until meeting the Ouse at Nun Monkton, seven miles above York. Pateley Bridge is the main centre of the upper dale, and Knaresborough, a fine market town, has all amenities for the tourist and holiday-maker, with the resort of Harrogate near to it.

The Nidd rises at 2,000 feet on Great Whernside at Nidd Head. The bare fells sweep down to the Angram and Scar House reservoirs, which were built by Bradford Corporation. Work started on these before the first world war, and thousands of men laboured on them. A light railway ran from Pateley Bridge, joining there with the L.N.E.R. line from Harrogate, until it was dismantled in 1936. A private road was built from Lofthouse to the reservoirs, and this is open to the public on summer weekends. The dam at Scar House is 1,800 feet long and 170 feet high. Two miles below this where the valley turns sharply to the south, is a tunnel cut into the rock for the railway. Just below here the Nidd disappears underground at Manchester Hole, with the overflow going down nearby Goyden Pot. Sudden flooding makes these potholes very dangerous, and they should not be entered without expert guidance and equipment. The Nidd emerges near the village of:

Lofthouse. 7m Pateley Bridge; also narrow road to Masham (10m). This small village climbs up the hillside from the dale road, at the junction of which is the old station on the light railway. There are some cottages and a fountain, and from the field at the top of the village a green road runs up the dale from the steep Masham road. The monks of Fountains Abbey had a grange here. Iron mining has left a few scars on the hillside.

Inn: The Crown.
Post Office and Shop.
Buses: West Yorkshire from Pateley Bridge.
Caravans: Studfold Farm, T, MC.

Middlesmoor. 900 feet up, on a ridge of moorland, Middlesmoor offers splendid views. From the churchyard, the scene down to Gouthwaite and Pateley Bridge is one that attracts many photographers. The tiny village is across the dale from Lofthouse, and is reached by a steep road with a hairpin bend. A track from the head of the village leads to Scar House. The church is of 13th century origins but is largely 19th century; it contains the cross of St. Chad, A.D. 664.

Inn: The Crown.
Buses: West Yorkshire from Pateley Bridge.
Between Lofthouse and Middlesmoor, a lane leads off to:

How Stean, a spectacular limestone gorge with caves and waterfalls. After crossing the bridge over the beck, there is a car park and cafe. The path crosses the stream by rustic bridges and follows narrow waterworn ledges above the torrent. In Tom Taylor's cave, 32 silver Roman coins were found in 1868. There are stalactites in Eglin's Hole, and waterfalls at Park Foss and Cliff Foss. Care should be taken after rain as the paths are slippery.

Ramsgill. 4m from Pateley Bridge. A charming little place, it has a creeper-covered inn across a well kept green, old cottages next to the beck and a church which looks down the two miles expanse of Gouthwaite. The Yorke Arms, formerly a shooting lodge for the land-owning family, was rebuilt in 1843 about the same time as the church of St. Mary the Virgin was erected. Near this are the remains of a chapel built by the monks of Byland, who had a grange here. Eugene Aram, the murderer whose story was used by Thomas Hood and Bulwer Lytton, was born in Ramsgill in 1704. *The Dalesman* oak seat on the green was awarded in the Best Kept Village Competition a few years ago.

Inn: The Yorke Arms.
Youth Hostel (Longside House).
Buses from Pateley Bridge.

Across the river at Bouthwaite, which is a hamlet on the site of another monastic grange belonging to Fountains, is a waterfall in Lul Beck.

Gouthwaite. This reservoir, a haunt of wild fowl, is for compensation purposes. Beneath its waters once stood Gouthwaite Hall, the seat of the Yorke family before they moved to Bewerley Hall, near Pateley Bridge. The mullioned windows were incorporated in the new hall which stands near the road alongside the water.

Wath. Just below the dam and the trees which conceal it, a road crosses the river by a narrow packhorse bridge, built by monks from Fountains, and enters the tiny village of Wath. It is a peaceful place, with many trees and a waterfall in the woods. The road continues on the hillside into Pateley Bridge.

Inn: The Sportsman's Arms.
Buses from Pateley Bridge stop at the bridge.

On the main dale road, nearer Pateley, is Foster Beck Mill — now an inn — with its huge waterwheel. This provided power for rope-making. Merryfield Gill near here has relics of lead-mining days, and there is a caravan site here. Just before reaching Pateley, there is a caravan site next to the recreation ground. The road joins the steep B6265 which climbs to Greenhow and Grassington.

PATELEY BRIDGE

B6165 to Harrogate (14m). B6265 to Ripon (11m). The main centre of upper Nidderdale, the old town of Pateley Bridge has a steep narrow main street running up from the river. It used to be cobbled, and on Pateley Show day it is thronged with farm vehicles. In lead-mining days it was even busier. The railway is closed now, but buses link with Harrogate and Ripon, and many people who work in these towns live here.

Pateley's market charter was granted in the 14th century. Its name in Domesday is 'Neresford,' but its present name may have some connection with the old name 'pate,' or badger, although this is disputed by some authorities. Across the river is a pleasant park, with swings and slides for the children (also tennis and bowls), and there are many walks on the hillsides. High above the town are the ruins of the old church of St. Mary. These can be reached by the steps, just to the right at the top of the High Street, which leads to Panorama Walk, giving fine views of the dale and across to Yorke's Folly. These two towers (or 'stoops') were built by the Yorke family to provide employment at a time of industrial depression.

To the left of the High Street, when coming up from the river, is the church of St. Cuthbert, built in the 19th century. Here is a medieval church bell, believed to have come from Fountains Abbey after the Dissolution, and used until 1893. Although much of the old property in Pateley has been altered or demolished, there are some fine houses in the narrow streets. Lead-mining was once the main occupation of the inhabitants and, when the railway came, stone from a quarry was taken down to it by an inclined tramway. There is a museum in the council offices on the hill above the bus station.

Nidderdale Agricultural Society's annual show on the last Monday in September is one of the most important in the dales. It was started in 1846, and is held across the river in Bewerley Park. This was originally part of the estate of the Yorke family, who were lords of the manor.

Population: **1,600.**

Early Closing: Thursday.

Inns: Talbot. King's Head.

Several shops, post office, cafes, banks, etc.

Buses from Harrogate, Ripon and Grassington (weekends).

Car park and toilets, just off the High Street.

Caravans: Riverside Caravan Park, T, MC. Heathfield Caravan Park, T. Fell Beck Caravan Park (B6265), T, MC. Westfield, Merryfield Glen, T, MC. Low Wood (B6165), T, MC.

Garages.

Angling tickets from most hotels.

Bewerley. This village is across the river from Pateley, and the road through it enters Glasshouses, passing a mill dam and climbing up to the main road from Pateley to Harrogate. In Bewerley is the camp school organised by the county education authority. Just off the road is the beautiful Grange chapel, a restored medieval building in a quiet garden. The road to Yorke's Folly climbs out of Bewerley. It is very steep, and from Guise Cliff there are magnificent views extending from Great Whernside to York Minster. In the wood below the mile-long cliff is Guise Cliff Tarn, and several unusual rocks and caves with names such as the Giant's Chair, the Needle's Eye and the Crocodile Rock. A small valley, just before the bridge in Bewerley, is a delightful place for a walk.

Greenhow. The scattered, isolated hamlet was a lead-mining community. At 1,275 feet, it has a church which is probably the highest situated place of worship in England. Low cloud often wreathes the place, but on clear sunny days the views back over Nidderdale are splendid. The road from Bewerley climbs very steeply for a couple of miles, passing a quarry and then the old burial ground and the inn, to reach the church. Duck Street leads off left to Blubber-houses and Thruscross. Lead-mining was carried on here by the Romans, and pigs of lead with their inscriptions have been found. The industry ceased at the end of the 19th century, but the surrounding moorland is pitted with abandoned workings and dangerous mine shafts.

Inn: The Miner's Arms.

Post Office.

Bus from Pateley Bridge and Grassington (weekends).

Stump Cross Cavern. This fascinating underground wonderland, with its stalactites and coloured rock formations, is said to be one of the finest in the country. It is lit by electricity and can be explored in safety; it is on the Grassington road from Greenhow and is open daily.

Brimham Rocks. On the north side of Nidderdale, about 3½m from Pateley Bridge, the rocks can be reached from the Ripon road, B6265, or from Summerbridge on the B6165. This collection of weird-shaped rocks at nearly a thousand feet is one of the best examples of wind erosion in Britain. The millstone grit has been sculptured by the elements into fantastic shapes. The biggest, the Idol Rock, weighs 200 tons, yet it rests on a pedestal only 12 inches wide. Some of the huge blocks can be rocked by hand, and others have holes in them.

'Open daily. Car park, cafe and toilets. National Trust museum and shop.

Lower Nidderdale. The dale gradually widens and loses its wildness, and has many trees and several interesting villages. Some of these were developed in the 19th century, when small mills expanded the textile industry. All have interesting corners, old houses and inns. They include Dacre, Darley, Summerbridge, Birstwith, Burnt Yates, Hampsthwaite and, off to the west, Thruscross, where the reservoir is colourful at weekends with yachts.

Ripley. 10m Pateley Bridge. This charming village with its castle is by-passed by the main road. The castle, the home of the Ingilby family, is a Tudor building on the site of a feudal fortress, with many interesting relics. Cromwell stayed here after the battle of Marston Moor, and the church wall is marked with the bullets of his soldiers. The castle is open to the public at certain times.

KNARESBOROUGH

A59, 4m from A1. This ancient Royal Borough stands on the bank of a gorge, where the Nidd has carved out the magnesium limestone. Quite different to the places in the upper dale, Knaresborough has red roofed houses climbing the side of the gorge, which is topped by the ruined castle. The 15th century prophetess, Mother Shipton, lived in a cave across the river and, at the Dropping Well, articles hung under the limestone cliff are transformed into stone by the spring waters. Under the arches of the railway viaduct the river is thronged with boats and punts. Near the river bridge is a public park, Conyngham Hall, with fine trees and grassland. Here there is also a zoo, putting greens and tennis courts.

There are car parks, many shops, inns, cafes, garages and a caravan site, and the old town is a good centre for touring. Rail and bus connections to York and Harrogate.

Angling: Tickets from Mr. P. Smith, High Street.

Harrogate. The elegant spa town is only three miles from Knaresborough. Although not in Nidderdale, it is near enough to be of interest to dales' visitors seeking all the amenities of a busy community, with beautiful open spaces, gardens and entertainments. There are main road and rail links with principal cities.

BOOKS

Nidderdale; Knaresborough Castle (both Dalesman Publishing Company).